Positive Parenting in the Christian Home

A Faith-Based Guide to Raising Compassionate, Confident, and Christ-Centered Children

© Tiffany Barker

Table of Contents

Introduction

Purpose of the Book

Parenting is both one of the toughest and most fulfilling roles a person can have. For Christian parents, this task is intertwined with their faith, aiming not only to guide their children through life but to shape their hearts and minds in alignment with Christian values. The goal of this book is to provide a practical and faith-based approach to parenting that helps parents nurture their children into compassionate, confident, and Christ-centered individuals.

In this book, you'll find guidance rooted in Christian teachings and principles. We aim to offer practical advice and actionable steps that align with your faith. We will explore methods and strategies that emphasize love, respect, and understanding, ensuring that your parenting journey is both fulfilling and deeply rooted in your Christian beliefs.

This book is designed to be a resource you can turn to at any stage of your parenting journey. Whether you are just beginning or have been parenting for years, the principles and strategies outlined here will help you reinforce your faith while fostering a positive and loving environment for your children.

Discuss the Importance of Positive Parenting Within a Christian Framework

Positive parenting is more than just a method; it's a way of life that encourages the development of a child's character and emotional well-being. In a Christian framework, positive parenting involves nurturing a child's growth in ways that reflect the love and teachings of Jesus Christ. This approach is built on the foundation of respect, empathy, and guidance that aligns with Christian values.

Incorporating positive parenting techniques within a Christian context means emphasizing the importance of love and grace in your interactions with your children. It means modeling behavior that reflects your faith, such as kindness, patience, and forgiveness. This method encourages parents to respond to their children's needs with understanding and support, rather than resorting to punishment or negativity.

A positive Christian parenting approach helps children develop a strong sense of self-worth and confidence, knowing they are loved unconditionally and supported in their faith journey. It also fosters an environment where children feel safe to explore their beliefs and grow spiritually. By applying these principles, parents can create a nurturing home where their children can thrive both emotionally and spiritually.

positive parenting within a Christian framework is about creating a loving and supportive environment that reflects your faith. It involves guiding your children with kindness and understanding, modeling Christian values, and fostering their growth in a way that aligns with your beliefs. This approach not only helps in raising well-rounded individuals but also strengthens the bond between parent and child through shared faith and values.

Address Common Challenges Faced by Christian Parents Today

Parenting today presents a unique set of challenges, especially for Christian parents who are committed to raising their children in line with their faith. One of the major hurdles is balancing modern life with traditional Christian values. In a world where secular influences are pervasive, maintaining a Christ-centered approach can be difficult. Parents often find themselves navigating a landscape filled with conflicting messages and pressures from society, media, and peers.

Another challenge is managing the digital age's impact on children. Technology, while beneficial in many ways, also introduces new issues such as screen time, online safety, and exposure to inappropriate content. Christian parents must find ways to integrate their faith into discussions about technology, ensuring their children use it responsibly and safely.

Additionally, many parents struggle with time management and maintaining a healthy family dynamic amidst busy schedules. With the demands of work, school, and extracurricular activities, finding quality time for family and faith can be challenging. This often leads to stress and a feeling of inadequacy, as parents try to balance their responsibilities while ensuring they nurture their children's spiritual and emotional growth.

Financial pressures are also a significant concern. Economic constraints can limit access to resources or activities that support Christian values, such as attending church events or participating in faith-based programs. Parents may struggle with how to provide for their families while adhering to their values and supporting their children's spiritual development.

Lastly, Christian parents may face difficulties in addressing moral and ethical issues that arise in their children's lives. Teaching children to navigate complex social situations, peer pressure, and personal dilemmas while remaining true to their faith requires careful thought and guidance.

Introduce the Key Themes of the Book: Compassion, Confidence, and Christ-Centered Living.

Amidst of these challenges, this book focuses on three key themes that are essential for positive parenting within a Christian framework: compassion, confidence, and Christ-centered living.

Compassion is the cornerstone of nurturing a child's emotional and spiritual well-being. It involves teaching children to be empathetic and understanding, modeling Christ's love through actions and words. Compassion in parenting means addressing your child's needs with kindness, listening to their concerns, and guiding them with patience and understanding. By fostering compassion, you help your children develop a heart that is open to others and rooted in Christian love.

Confidence is about helping children develop a strong sense of self-worth and assurance in their identity as beloved children of God. This theme involves encouraging children to explore their talents, face challenges with faith, and embrace their uniqueness. Building confidence in a Christian context means affirming their value through God's eyes, providing them with the tools to handle life's ups and downs with grace and courage.

Christ-Centered Living is the foundation upon which the other themes rest. It involves integrating Christian values into daily life, ensuring that your parenting reflects your faith in every aspect. Christ-centered living means guiding your children to understand and live out their faith, making choices that honor God, and creating a home environment that mirrors Christian teachings. It is about embedding spiritual practices into everyday routines and helping your children grow in their relationship with Christ.

By focusing on compassion, confidence, and Christ-centered living, this book aims to provide a comprehensive guide for Christian parents. These themes are not just ideals but practical principles that can be woven into daily parenting practices, offering a path to raising children who are emotionally healthy, confident, and grounded in their faith.

Why Positive Parenting?

A positive parenting approach offers numerous benefits that extend beyond immediate child behavior and impact a child's long-term development. This method focuses on nurturing and guiding rather than punishing, creating a supportive environment where children feel loved and respected.

One of the primary benefits of positive parenting is the development of a strong, trusting relationship between parent and child. When parents use positive reinforcement, children learn to associate their behavior with approval and encouragement rather than fear of punishment. This approach fosters open communication, where children feel comfortable expressing their thoughts and emotions, knowing they will be heard and understood.

Positive parenting also enhances a child's emotional and social skills. By modeling and teaching behaviors such as empathy, kindness, and problem-solving, parents help their children develop healthy interpersonal relationships and navigate social situations effectively. This approach equips children with the tools they need to handle challenges with confidence and resilience.

Moreover, positive parenting contributes to a child's self-esteem and self-worth. When children receive praise for their efforts and achievements, they build a sense of accomplishment and confidence. This positive reinforcement encourages them to take on new challenges and pursue their goals with enthusiasm, knowing their parents support and believe in their abilities.

Additionally, a positive parenting approach supports better behavioral outcomes. By focusing on encouraging desirable behaviors and providing consistent, loving guidance, parents can reduce instances of negative behavior and conflict. This method promotes a harmonious family environment where children learn to self-regulate and make positive choices.

Brief Overview of the Role of Faith in Parenting

Incorporating faith into parenting adds a profound layer of meaning and guidance to the parenting process. Faith provides a moral and spiritual framework that shapes how parents interact with their children and address various aspects of their development.

For Christian parents, faith offers a foundation for teaching values such as love, forgiveness, and integrity. By aligning parenting practices with Christian teachings, parents model behaviors and attitudes that reflect their beliefs. This helps children understand and embrace these values, integrating them into their own lives.

Faith also provides parents with strength and guidance during challenging times. Relying on prayer and biblical principles helps parents navigate difficulties with grace and patience. It offers a sense of purpose and reassurance that they are not alone in their parenting journey, fostering a supportive environment for both parents and children.

Additionally, faith encourages the development of a child's spiritual growth. By introducing children to religious practices, such as prayer, Bible study, and worship, parents help them build a relationship with God. This spiritual foundation supports their emotional and moral development, guiding them in making decisions that align with their faith.

Overall, positive parenting and faith complement each other by providing a framework for nurturing a child's emotional, social, and spiritual well-being. While positive parenting fosters a loving and supportive environment, faith adds depth and purpose to the parenting process, guiding both parents and children in their journey together.

Part 1

Building a Christ-Centered Foundation.

Chapter 1

Understanding Christian Parenting

Christian parenting goes beyond traditional parenting approaches by integrating faith deeply into every aspect of raising children. It's about more than just teaching right from wrong; it's about guiding your children to grow up with a strong sense of Christian values and principles that will shape their entire lives.

Defining Christian Parenting

At its core, Christian parenting is about nurturing your children in a way that reflects God's love and teachings. It means raising your children with the understanding that their lives are part of a greater spiritual journey. Christian parenting focuses on more than just academic or behavioral success; it aims to cultivate a deep and lasting relationship with God.

Christian parenting involves setting an example through your actions. It means living out the values you wish to instill in your children. This might look like showing kindness and forgiveness in your everyday interactions, or it could involve making time for prayer and Bible study as a family. By demonstrating these values, you provide a living example of what it means to follow Christ.

Principles of Christian Parenting

1. Unconditional Love: One of the foundational principles of Christian parenting is showing unconditional love. Just as God loves us despite our flaws, parents are encouraged to love their children without conditions. This love helps children feel secure and valued, and it sets the stage for them to understand and embrace God's love.

2. Modeling Faith: Children learn by observing their parents. By actively practicing your faith, you provide a model for your children to follow. This includes regular participation in church activities, personal prayer, and discussions about your beliefs. When children see their parents living out their faith, it helps them understand its importance and encourages them to adopt similar practices.

3. Guidance and Instruction: Christian parenting involves guiding your children in making choices that reflect Christian values. This means teaching them about right and wrong according to biblical principles and helping them apply these teachings in their daily lives. It's about offering wisdom and instruction that helps them navigate the complexities of life while staying true to their faith.

4. Discipline with Love: Discipline in Christian parenting is not about punishment but about correction and growth. It's about guiding your children in a loving manner, helping them understand the consequences of their actions while offering forgiveness and support. This approach helps children learn from their mistakes and grow in character, all while feeling loved and valued.

5. Encouraging Spiritual Growth: Christian parenting includes nurturing your children's spiritual growth. This can be achieved through activities like family prayer, Bible reading, and attending church together. It's important to engage with your children about their spiritual questions and encourage them to develop their own relationship with God.

6. Prayer and Reflection: Incorporating prayer and reflection into daily life is crucial in Christian parenting. Prayer helps to connect with God, seek guidance, and express gratitude. It also serves as a powerful tool for addressing challenges and seeking support. Encouraging children to pray and reflect helps them develop a personal relationship with God and strengthens their faith.

7. Community and Fellowship: Being part of a Christian community provides support and reinforces the values taught at home. Involvement in church activities and fellowship with other believers offers children a broader perspective on their faith and helps them build relationships with other Christians.

By understanding and applying these principles, Christian parents can create a nurturing environment that supports their children's spiritual, emotional, and moral development. This approach not only helps children grow in their faith but also prepares them to face life's challenges with a strong Christian foundation.

The Biblical Basis for Parenting

The Bible offers rich guidance for parenting, providing timeless principles that help shape a Christ-centered approach to raising children. Drawing from the King James Version (KJV) of the Bible, these scriptures offer foundational truths and practical wisdom for Christian parents.

The book of Proverbs provides significant insight into the role of parents. Proverbs 22:6 (KJV) states, "Train up a child in the way he should go: and when he is old, he will not depart from it." This verse highlights the significance of guiding children on the right path from an early age. It suggests that early, consistent teaching and nurturing will have a lasting impact on their lives, leading them to hold onto these values as they grow older.

Discipline is another key aspect highlighted in the Bible. Proverbs 13:24 (KJV) says, "He that spareth his rod hateth his son: but he that loveth him chasteneth him betimes." This verse underscores that discipline, when applied with love, is an essential part of parenting. It's about correcting and guiding children to help them learn and grow, not about punishment. The focus is on loving guidance that helps children understand the consequences of their actions and develop self-control.

The Bible also speaks to the importance of modeling godly behavior. Ephesians 6:4 (KJV) instructs, "And, ye fathers, provoke not your children to wrath: but bring them up in the nurture and admonition of the Lord." This verse highlights the need for parents to raise their children in a manner that reflects God's teachings. It encourages parents to provide gentle, loving guidance rather than provoking anger, ensuring that the child's upbringing is rooted in Christian values.

Teaching children about God and His commandments is another vital aspect of biblical parenting. Deuteronomy 6:6-7 (KJV) states, "And these words, which I command thee this day, shall be in thine heart: And thou shalt teach them diligently unto thy children, and shalt talk of them when thou sittest in thine house, and when thou walkest by the way, and when thou liest down, and when thou risest up." This passage explain the importance of making God's teachings an integral part of daily life. It encourages parents to consistently discuss and teach their children about God's commands, integrating these lessons into every aspect of life.

In addition to teaching and discipline, the Bible emphasizes the role of love in parenting. 1 Corinthians 13:4-7 (KJV) describes the nature of love, stating, "Love suffereth long, and is kind; love envieth not; love vaunteth not itself, is not puffed up, Doth not behave itself unseemly, seeketh not her own, is not easily provoked, thinketh no evil; Rejoiceth not in iniquity, but rejoiceth in the truth; Beareth all things, believeth all things, hopeth all things, endureth all things." These verses depict love as patient, kind, and enduring—qualities that are essential in parenting. By embodying these traits, parents can create a loving and supportive environment that encourages children to thrive.

Finally, Psalm 127:3 (KJV) reminds us of the blessing of children: "Lo, children are an heritage of the Lord: and the fruit of the womb is his reward." This verse acknowledges that children are a gift from God and a valuable part of His plan. It serves as a reminder for parents to cherish and value their role in raising these precious gifts, understanding that parenting is both a privilege and a responsibility.

By grounding parenting practices in these biblical principles, Christian parents can build a strong foundation for nurturing their children. These scriptures provide a guide for raising children in a way that reflects God's love and teachings, ensuring that parenting efforts align with divine wisdom and purpose.

The Role of Faith in Daily Parenting Practices

Faith plays a central role in shaping how Christian parents approach daily parenting practices. It influences how they interact with their children, make decisions, and manage family life. Integrating faith into everyday activities helps create a home environment that reflects Christian values and nurtures the spiritual growth of both parents and children.

One way faith impacts daily parenting is through the practice of prayer. Regular family prayers help center the family on God and invite His guidance into everyday decisions. Starting or ending the day with prayer sets a spiritual tone, encouraging children to communicate with God about their thoughts and concerns. It also provides an opportunity for parents to model trust in God's provision and wisdom.

Bible reading is another essential practice in faith-based parenting. Incorporating Bible stories or verses into daily routines helps children learn about God's teachings and how they apply to everyday situations. Reading Scripture together encourages discussions about moral lessons and how to live according to God's word. This practice not only strengthens the family's spiritual foundation but also helps children develop a deeper understanding of their faith.

Faith also influences how parents handle challenges and conflicts within the family. When faced with difficulties, Christian parents turn to their faith for strength and guidance. By relying on biblical principles, they approach problems with a perspective that seeks solutions in alignment with God's will. This approach teaches children to handle their own challenges with faith and resilience.

Modeling Christian behavior in daily life is another significant aspect of integrating faith into parenting. Children learn by observing their parents, so demonstrating values like patience, forgiveness, and humility is crucial. When parents react to situations with kindness and grace, they provide a living example of how faith influences behavior. This modeling helps children internalize these values and apply them in their own interactions.

Faith also shapes how parents approach discipline. Christian parenting emphasizes discipline that is rooted in love and guidance rather than punishment. By using biblical principles to correct and instruct, parents help children understand the purpose of discipline and its role in their growth. This approach ensures that discipline is constructive and aligned with God's teachings.

Additionally, faith impacts family activities and traditions. Incorporating spiritual practices into family life, such as attending church together or participating in community service, reinforces the importance of faith. These activities provide opportunities for the family to bond while actively living out Christian values.

Overall, faith is interwoven into every aspect of daily parenting. It guides how parents interact with their children, make decisions, and handle challenges. By integrating faith into daily practices, Christian parents create a home environment that reflects God's love and teachings, fostering spiritual growth and a deep connection with their faith.

Chapter 2
Creating a Godly Home Environment

Creating a home that reflects Christian values involves more than just occasional acts of faith; It's about integrating these values into the core of daily life. A Godly home environment is one where faith influences every aspect of family life, from daily routines to the way challenges are handled.

Start by creating a physical space in the home that encourages spiritual growth can also be beneficial. Set up a corner or room dedicated to prayer and reflection. This could include a small table with a Bible, a journal, and perhaps some inspirational artwork or quotes. Having a dedicated space for spiritual activities makes it easier for family members to focus on their faith and provides a visual reminder of its importance.

Incorporate Christian values into daily routines. For example, make saying grace before meals a family tradition. This simple act of gratitude helps to acknowledge God's provision and reminds everyone of the importance of thankfulness. Similarly, use family gatherings and events as opportunities to reflect on Christian teachings. Whether it's a holiday celebration or a casual family dinner, integrate faith-based discussions and practices into these moments.

Modeling Christian behavior is crucial. Children learn a great deal by observing their parents. Show them how to handle conflicts with grace and patience. Demonstrate forgiveness in your interactions and model humility in your everyday actions. When kids see their parents living out Christian values, they're more likely to adopt those behaviors themselves.

Encourage your children to develop their own faith practices. This might include helping them establish their own prayer routines or encouraging them to read the Bible on their own. Provide them with age-appropriate Christian resources, such as devotional books or faith-based activities, that they can engage with independently. Supporting their personal faith journey helps them develop a deeper connection with God.

Create traditions that reinforce Christian teachings. Celebrate religious holidays and milestones with activities that highlight their spiritual significance. For example, during Christmas, focus on the story of Jesus' birth and incorporate activities that reflect this message. During Easter, discuss the resurrection of Christ and its importance. These traditions help to keep the focus on faith and make it a central part of family life.

Address conflicts and challenges with a faith-based perspective. When disagreements arise, approach them with a mindset of seeking resolution through love and understanding. Use these moments as opportunities to teach children about forgiveness, patience, and empathy. By handling conflicts in a way that reflects Christian principles, you help reinforce the values you wish to instill in your children.

Finally, be intentional about the influence of external media and activities on your family. Choose books, movies, and entertainment that align with Christian values and avoid those that might contradict them. This careful selection helps ensure that the external influences your children are exposed to are consistent with the values you are teaching at home.

By integrating these practices into your family life, you create a home environment that reflects Christian values and nurtures spiritual growth. This environment supports the development of compassionate, confident, and Christ-centered children who understand and embrace their faith in their daily lives.

Establishing routines

Establishing routines that include prayer, Bible study, and worship helps embed these practices into the everyday life of your family, creating a rhythm that keeps faith central in all activities.

Begin by setting a regular time for family prayer. Choose a time that fits your family's schedule, whether it's in the morning to start the day, before meals, or at bedtime. Gather together as a family to pray, sharing your concerns, hopes, and thanks to God. Keep the prayers simple and sincere, allowing each person to contribute according to their comfort level. This routine helps to center the family around faith and makes prayer a natural part of daily life.

Incorporate Bible study into your daily or weekly routine. Select a specific time for reading Scripture together, such as after dinner or before bedtime. Use a Bible that is accessible for all family members, including children, and choose passages that are relevant to their lives. Discuss the readings as a family, encouraging everyone to share their thoughts and how the verses apply to their daily experiences. This practice helps to deepen your family's understanding of the Bible and reinforces its teachings in everyday situations.

Include worship in your routine as well. Play Christian music or hymns during family activities like mealtimes or while getting ready for the day. Singing or listening to worship songs together helps to cultivate a worshipful atmosphere and reminds everyone of God's presence. Attend church services regularly as a family and engage in worship activities with your community. This regular participation in corporate worship strengthens your family's faith and provides opportunities to connect with others who share your beliefs.

Create additional opportunities for faith-based activities throughout the week. For example, use car rides or free time to listen to Christian podcasts or audio Bible readings. These moments provide a chance to keep faith discussions going even when you're not gathered as a family. Encourage each family member to develop their own personal prayer and Bible study routines as well, supporting their individual spiritual growth.

Having visual reminders of faith around the home can also support these routines. Display Bible verses, religious symbols, or inspirational quotes in common areas. These reminders can prompt prayer, reflection, and discussions about faith, helping to keep spiritual practices a regular part of daily life.

By integrating these routines into your family's daily life, you create a consistent and meaningful way to keep faith at the center of your home. Prayer, Bible study, and worship become natural parts of your family's rhythm, fostering spiritual growth and strengthening your connection with God.

The influence of parents as spiritual leaders.

Parents have a profound influence as spiritual leaders within their families. They set the tone for the spiritual climate of the home through their actions, attitudes, and commitment to faith. By embodying the principles of Christianity, parents provide a powerful example that shapes their children's understanding of faith.

The way parents live out their faith speaks volumes. Children observe how their parents handle everyday situations, conflicts, and challenges. When parents respond with patience, forgiveness, and love, they model Christian values in action. This everyday demonstration of faith helps children learn how to apply these values in their own lives. The consistency between what parents teach and how they live reinforces the credibility of their faith and encourages children to adopt similar behaviors.

Parents also serve as spiritual mentors to their children. This role involves guiding them in their spiritual journey, providing support, and offering wisdom. Engaging in regular spiritual practices together, such as prayer, Bible study, and worship, helps parents teach their children about God's teachings and how to live according to them. By taking an active role in their children's spiritual development, parents help lay a strong foundation for their faith.

Modeling a personal relationship with God is crucial. Parents who actively seek to deepen their own faith through prayer, study, and worship demonstrate the importance of a personal connection with God. This personal example can inspire children to develop their own relationship with God, understanding that faith is a personal journey rather than just a set of rules.

Handling family conflicts and challenges with a faith-centered approach is another way parents influence their children spiritually. When parents address issues with grace, seek reconciliation, and rely on God's guidance, they show their children how to approach difficulties in a manner consistent with Christian teachings. This approach helps children learn how to navigate their own challenges with faith and resilience.

Additionally, parents can foster a spiritual environment by encouraging their children to participate in faith-based activities. Involve them in church events, community service, and other activities that reflect Christian values. By engaging in these activities as a family, parents help their children see faith as an active and integral part of life.

The influence of parents as spiritual leaders is also evident in how they prioritize faith in family life. Making time for spiritual practices, discussing faith openly, and celebrating religious milestones reinforces the importance of faith. These practices show children that faith is not just a part of Sunday worship but a guiding force in everyday life.

Ultimately, parents' roles as spiritual leaders are about living out their faith in a way that inspires and guides their children. By being consistent in their values, actively participating in their children's spiritual growth, and demonstrating a genuine relationship with God, parents provide a model for their children to follow. This influence shapes their children's understanding of faith and helps them develop a strong, personal connection with God.

Chapter 3
Nurturing Faith in Your Children

Nurturing faith in your children is a journey that starts early and evolves as they grow. Each stage of a child's development offers unique opportunities to introduce and deepen their understanding of faith. Tailoring your approach to their age helps make faith accessible and engaging for them.

For infants and toddlers, focus on creating a loving and secure environment where faith is naturally woven into daily routines. Start with simple, positive reinforcement of faith values. Sing Christian songs, read Bible stories, and model behaviors like kindness and love. Infants and toddlers absorb these experiences through repetition and observation. Use colorful Bible storybooks and gentle prayers to introduce them to the concept of God's love and care.

As children enter their preschool years, begin to introduce them to basic biblical stories and concepts. Use interactive methods such as picture books and simple Bible stories with engaging illustrations. Encourage their curiosity by answering their questions about God and faith in ways they can understand. At this stage, children are learning about relationships and emotions, so emphasize stories that teach values like kindness, sharing, and forgiveness.

In the early elementary years, children start to grasp more complex ideas. This is a good time to introduce them to the broader narrative of the Bible. Use age-appropriate children's Bibles or devotional books that offer simple explanations of Bible stories and moral lessons. Engage them with activities that relate to the stories, such as crafts or role-playing. Encourage them to share what they learn and ask questions, which helps reinforce their understanding and allows them to connect their faith with their everyday experiences.

As children grow into the later elementary years, they begin to develop their own understanding of faith and its implications for their lives. This is a key time to deepen their Bible knowledge and encourage personal reflection. Involve them in family Bible study, where they can participate in discussions and share their thoughts. Provide them with their own Bible that includes study aids or devotionals geared toward their age group. Encourage them to start their own personal prayer and Bible reading habits, supporting them with tools like prayer journals or age-appropriate devotionals.

During adolescence, teens are exploring their identity and values. It is crucial to support their spiritual development while respecting their growing independence. Engage in open and honest discussions about faith, addressing their doubts and questions with empathy and understanding. Encourage them to be involved in youth groups or church activities where they can connect with peers who share their beliefs. Provide guidance and support as they develop their own personal relationship with God and make faith their own.

Throughout all stages, maintain an open dialogue about faith. Encourage your children to express their thoughts, struggles, and discoveries about God. This ongoing communication helps them feel supported and valued in their spiritual journey. Model a life of faith and demonstrate how it influences your decisions and actions. Your example provides a living testament to the values and beliefs you wish to impart to your children.

By adapting your approach to fit your child's developmental stage, you create a nurturing environment where faith can grow and flourish. Each stage offers unique opportunities to introduce and deepen your child's understanding of Christianity, helping them develop a strong and personal connection with their faith.

Teaching children about Jesus and the Bible.

Teaching children about Jesus and the Bible involves making the stories and teachings accessible and engaging at each stage of their development. Start with the basics and build a foundation that helps them understand and connect with their faith.

Begin by introducing the figure of Jesus in a way that resonates with young children. Use simple language to explain who Jesus is, focusing on His love, kindness, and the miracles He performed. Picture books and storybooks that highlight Jesus' life and teachings can be very effective. Read these stories together, discussing the key messages and how they apply to everyday life. Emphasize the aspects of Jesus' character that children can relate to, such as His compassion and care for others.

For preschoolers and early elementary children, use engaging and interactive methods to teach Bible stories. Storytelling can be enhanced with visual aids like illustrations or puppets that bring the characters and events to life. Interactive activities such as crafts or songs related to Bible stories can help reinforce the lessons. For example, after reading about the Good Shepherd, you might create a shepherd craft or sing songs about Jesus as the shepherd. These activities make the stories memorable and help children connect with the teachings on a personal level.

As children progress to later elementary years, introduce them to more detailed Bible stories and their meanings. Use a children's Bible that provides explanations and context for the stories. Encourage them to read passages themselves and discuss what they understand from them. Engage in discussions about the life of Jesus, His teachings, and how they apply to their lives. For instance, talk about the Sermon on the Mount and its teachings on love and forgiveness, and how these can be practiced in their own lives.

For adolescents, focus on helping them make a personal connection with Jesus and the Bible. Encourage them to read and study the Bible on their own, using age-appropriate study guides or devotionals that help them explore its themes and messages more deeply. Discuss complex topics and encourage them to ask questions and express their thoughts. Engage in conversations about how Jesus' teachings can be applied to their current experiences and decisions. Providing them with opportunities to participate in discussions, youth groups, or service projects can help them see how their faith can be lived out in practical ways.

Throughout all stages, ensure that teaching about Jesus and the Bible is a two-way interaction. Encourage children to share their thoughts, ask questions, and express their understanding of the stories and teachings. Be open to their interpretations and guide them gently towards a deeper understanding. Modeling your own engagement with the Bible and your relationship with Jesus can inspire them to develop their own faith practices.

By making the stories and teachings of Jesus accessible and relevant to your child's developmental stage, you help them build a strong foundation of faith. This approach fosters a personal connection with Jesus and an understanding of His teachings, which can guide and support them throughout their lives.

Encouraging questions and exploration of faith.

Encouraging questions and exploration of faith helps children engage more deeply with their spiritual journey and build a strong foundation for their beliefs. When children ask questions about faith, it shows their curiosity and desire to understand more about their beliefs and the world around them. Embracing this curiosity creates opportunities for meaningful discussions and growth in their spiritual lives.

Start by creating an open environment where questions about faith are welcomed and valued. Let your children know that it's okay to ask questions and that their curiosity is a sign of their growing faith. Listen to their questions with patience and openness, providing thoughtful and age-appropriate answers. Avoid dismissing or simplifying their inquiries; instead, engage with them sincerely and explore the answers together.

Encourage children to ask questions not only about the basics of faith but also about complex or challenging topics. When they encounter difficulties understanding certain aspects of faith, offer to explore these questions together. Use age-appropriate resources such as Bible storybooks, devotionals, or educational materials that can provide additional insights. This collaborative approach helps them feel supported and valued in their quest for understanding.

Involve your children in discussions about faith-related issues and decisions. For example, when discussing a Bible story or a Christian principle, invite them to share their thoughts and perspectives. This practice helps them develop critical thinking skills and encourages them to form their own opinions about their faith. It also shows that their ideas are respected and considered valuable.

Encouraging exploration of faith also involves providing opportunities for children to engage in various aspects of their faith. Participate in church activities, attend Bible study groups, or join faith-based community service projects together. These experiences offer practical applications of their faith and help them see how it can be lived out in real life. By being actively involved in these activities, children gain a broader understanding of their faith and how it connects to their daily lives.

Support their exploration by allowing them to express their faith in creative ways. Encourage them to write, draw, or engage in activities that reflect their spiritual journey. For instance, they might create artwork that represents their understanding of a Bible story or write a journal entry about their faith experiences. These creative expressions help them process and articulate their beliefs in a personal and meaningful way.

When children face doubts or challenges in their faith, address these moments with empathy and encouragement. Offer guidance and support as they navigate their feelings and questions. Use these times as opportunities for growth and deeper understanding, rather than simply providing quick fixes. Reassure them that doubt is a normal part of the faith journey and that exploring these questions can lead to a stronger, more resilient faith.

By fostering an environment where questions are welcomed and exploration is encouraged, you help your children develop a robust and personal faith. This approach nurtures their curiosity, supports their spiritual growth, and builds a foundation for a lifelong relationship with their beliefs.

Part 2

Cultivating Compassion and Emotional Intelligence

Chapter 4
Raising Compassionate Children

Raising compassionate children is central to Christian parenting, as empathy and kindness are core values taught by Jesus. Compassion is more than just a feeling; it's an action that involves understanding and responding to the needs and feelings of others. Teaching children to be compassionate helps them connect with others and live out their faith in meaningful ways.

When you show compassion to others—whether it's helping a neighbor, volunteering, or listening to a friend in need—your children notice and learn from these examples. Share with them why you're taking certain actions and how they align with your faith values. Explain how Jesus demonstrated compassion and how we can follow His example in our own lives.

Encourage your children to express their feelings and understand the emotions of others. Create a safe space where they feel comfortable sharing their own experiences and emotions. This helps them develop emotional awareness and learn how to respond empathetically. For instance, if a friend is upset, talk with your child about how they might feel in that situation and discuss ways they can offer support or comfort.

Teach children to recognize and appreciate the feelings of those around them. Use everyday situations as opportunities to discuss emotions and empathy. When reading Bible stories or talking about people in the community, highlight moments where characters show kindness and understanding. Discuss how these actions can be applied in their own lives, such as being a good friend, showing respect to others, or helping those in need.

Make sure you involve your children in acts of kindness and service. Engaging in community service or helping others can provide practical lessons in compassion. Whether it's participating in a charity event, making care packages, or assisting with household chores, these activities teach children the value of contributing to the well-being of others. Explain the importance of these actions from a Christian perspective, emphasizing how serving others reflects Jesus' teachings.

Address conflicts and disagreements with compassion. When your child encounters problems with friends or family members, guide them through resolving issues with empathy and understanding. Encourage them to listen to others' perspectives and find solutions that consider everyone's feelings. This approach helps children practice empathy in real-life situations and strengthens their relationships with others.

Support your child's emotional development by encouraging them to develop self-awareness and self-regulation. Teach them to understand and manage their own emotions in healthy ways. Helping children identify their feelings and express them constructively lays the groundwork for empathizing with others. This might involve discussing their feelings during a difficult situation and finding positive ways to cope or solve problems.

Create opportunities for your children to learn about different experiences and cultures. Exposure to diverse perspectives broadens their understanding and fosters empathy towards people with different backgrounds. Engage in conversations about how people's experiences shape their feelings and needs, and discuss ways to show kindness and support.

Reinforce the value of compassion through positive reinforcement. Praise your children when they show empathy or kindness, and provide encouragement to continue these behaviors. Acknowledge their efforts and explain how their actions reflect the love and teachings of Jesus.

By integrating these practices into daily life, you help your children develop a deep sense of empathy and compassion. This foundation not only aligns with Christian teachings but also equips them to build meaningful and supportive relationships throughout their lives.

Teaching your children to love and serve others.

Teaching your children to love and serve others is a fundamental aspect of Christian parenting. It's about helping them understand the importance of selflessness and encouraging them to act on their faith by caring for those around them. This teaching starts at a young age and is reinforced through everyday actions and values.

Begin by modeling a loving and serving attitude in your own life. Children learn by observing, so let them see you practicing kindness and generosity. Whether it's helping a neighbor, volunteering at church, or simply showing compassion to those you encounter, your actions demonstrate what it means to live out your faith. Share with your children why you choose to help others and how it aligns with your beliefs, such as following Jesus' example of love and service.

Involve your children in service activities. Participate in community service projects together, such as food drives, clean-up events, or visiting the elderly. These experiences offer practical lessons in service and help children see the impact of their actions on others. When they are involved, they learn firsthand the joy and fulfillment that come from helping those in need.

Encourage acts of kindness within the family and community. Make it a habit to look for opportunities to serve others in your daily life. Encourage your children to think of ways they can help at home, such as setting the table, assisting with chores, or caring for a pet. Discuss how these small acts of service contribute to a loving and supportive environment. Recognize and celebrate their efforts to help others, reinforcing the value of these actions.

Teach your children to love and serve others by incorporating these principles into your family routines. For example, you can start a family tradition of praying for those in need or discussing ways to help others during family meals. Use these times to reflect on the importance of service and love in your faith and how your family can contribute to making a positive difference.

Discuss with your children the biblical teachings about loving and serving others. Share stories from the Bible that highlight Jesus' acts of service, such as washing His disciples' feet or feeding the hungry. Explain how these stories illustrate the call to serve others and how they can apply these teachings in their own lives.

Encourage empathy and understanding by discussing the needs and challenges faced by others. Talk about the struggles of people in different situations, whether they are facing financial difficulties, health issues, or personal hardships. Help your children understand how their actions can make a difference and encourage them to think of ways they can offer support or comfort.

Provide opportunities for your children to use their talents and skills to serve others. Whether they enjoy baking, crafting, or organizing, help them find ways to use their abilities to benefit others. For instance, they might bake cookies for a local charity, create handmade cards for the elderly, or help organize a community event. These activities not only teach them about service but also allow them to take pride in their contributions.

Reinforce the idea that serving others is not just about grand gestures but also about everyday actions. Remind your children that small acts of kindness, such as being a good friend, sharing with others, or showing respect, are all ways to love and serve those around them. By integrating these values into daily life, you help your children see that serving others is a natural and rewarding part of living out their faith.

Through consistent modeling, active involvement, and thoughtful discussions, you can teach your children to love and serve others. These lessons help them develop a deep sense of empathy and responsibility, aligning their actions with the teachings of Jesus and making a positive impact on their communities.

Practical ways to model and encourage compassion.

Modeling and encouraging compassion involves actively demonstrating empathy and kindness in everyday situations, creating an environment where these values are consistently practiced and celebrated. It starts with your actions and extends to the ways you guide and support your children in developing their own compassionate behaviors.

Begin by setting a personal example of compassion. Children are keen observers and often mimic the behaviors they see. Show empathy in your interactions with others, whether it's through a kind word, a helping hand, or simply listening attentively to someone's concerns. Let your children see you responding to others' needs with genuine care and concern. For instance, if a neighbor is struggling with groceries, involve your children in offering assistance, explaining how helping others aligns with your faith values.

Create opportunities for your children to practice compassion. Engage in activities that involve helping others, such as volunteering at a local shelter, participating in community clean-ups, or making care packages for those in need. Let your children take an active role in these activities, and discuss the impact of their contributions. This hands-on approach helps them understand the significance of their actions and see the real-world effects of compassion.

Encourage your children to express their feelings and respond to others' emotions. When a friend is sad or a family member is going through a tough time, discuss how they might offer support or comfort. Help them articulate their feelings and explore ways to be empathetic. For example, if a classmate is upset, talk about how they could offer a kind word or a friendly gesture to show they care.

Celebrate and reinforce compassionate behavior by acknowledging and praising your children's efforts. When they show empathy, such as sharing with a sibling or comforting a friend, provide positive reinforcement. Recognize their actions and explain how these behaviors reflect the love and teachings of Jesus. Praise helps them feel valued and encourages them to continue practicing compassion.

Use everyday situations as teaching moments. Discuss current events or personal experiences that highlight the need for compassion and empathy. For instance, if you hear about a natural disaster or a community member in need, talk with your children about how they might help or support those affected. Relate these discussions to biblical teachings and the importance of showing love and care for others.

Involve your children in planning and executing acts of kindness. Let them brainstorm ideas for helping others, such as organizing a charity event, making homemade gifts for a local hospital, or writing letters to elderly residents. Involving them in the planning process empowers them and helps them take ownership of their acts of service.

Foster a culture of empathy at home by regularly discussing feelings and emotions. Encourage open conversations about how each family member is feeling and how they might support one another. This practice helps children develop emotional intelligence and understand the importance of being considerate and supportive in their relationships.

Set up a compassion jar or a similar system where your family can track and celebrate acts of kindness. Each time someone performs a kind deed, write it down and add it to the jar. Periodically review the entries together and discuss the positive impact of these actions. This visual reminder reinforces the value of compassion and encourages ongoing efforts.

Lastly, be patient and consistent in your efforts to model and encourage compassion. Developing a compassionate mindset takes time and repetition. Continue to guide your children in understanding and practicing empathy, and provide gentle reminders of the importance of caring for others. Through consistent modeling, active involvement, and positive reinforcement, you help your children cultivate a lasting sense of compassion that aligns with their faith and enriches their interactions with the world.

Chapter 5
Emotional Intelligence in the Christian Home

Understanding and managing emotions within a Christian framework involves teaching children to recognize their feelings, respond to them in healthy ways, and align their emotional responses with their faith values. This approach helps children build emotional intelligence, which is crucial for their overall well-being and relationships with others.

Start by helping your children identify and name their emotions. Encourage them to express how they feel using simple terms such as happy, sad, angry, or frustrated. Use everyday situations as opportunities to talk about emotions. For instance, if they are upset about a disagreement with a friend, guide them in recognizing that emotion and discussing what might be causing it. This helps them develop self-awareness and understand their emotional responses.

Teach your children to manage their emotions by modeling appropriate responses. Show them how to handle frustration, disappointment, or anger in constructive ways. Instead of reacting with frustration when something goes wrong, demonstrate calmness and problem-solving. Explain how your faith guides your responses and how biblical teachings help you handle emotions. For example, you might refer to Proverbs 15:1, which says, "A soft answer turneth away wrath," to illustrate the importance of responding calmly.

Help your children understand that emotions are not inherently good or bad but are a natural part of being human. Teach them that it's okay to feel a wide range of emotions but that how they act on those feelings is important. Encourage them to express their feelings in ways that are respectful and constructive. For instance, if they are angry, suggest they take a few deep breaths or talk to someone they trust before reacting.

Incorporate prayer into emotional management. Encourage your children to turn to prayer when they are feeling overwhelmed or uncertain. Teach them that prayer can be a way to seek comfort, clarity, and strength. For instance, if they are anxious about a school event, guide them in praying for peace and confidence. This practice helps them rely on their faith to navigate their emotions and find solace in difficult times.

Use Bible stories and verses to illustrate how biblical characters dealt with their emotions. Discuss how figures like David or Jesus managed their feelings and how their faith influenced their responses. For example, you might talk about how David expressed his distress in the Psalms but ultimately trusted in God's plan. These stories provide practical examples of emotional management and reinforce the connection between faith and feelings.

Encourage your children to practice empathy and compassion in their interactions with others. Teach them to consider how others might feel and respond with kindness and understanding. For example, if a friend is going through a tough time, discuss how they might offer support and comfort. By practicing empathy, children learn to manage their own emotions in ways that build positive relationships and align with their Christian values.

Create a supportive space where your children feel safe to express their emotions. Let them know that it's okay to share their feelings with you and that you are there to listen and support them. Regularly check in with them about their emotional well-being and provide reassurance. This open communication helps them feel valued and understood, which is essential for emotional health.

Teach problem-solving skills as a way to manage emotions. When your children face challenges or conflicts, guide them in finding constructive solutions. Help them break down problems into manageable steps and explore different ways to address them. For instance, if they are struggling with a difficult assignment, work with them to develop a plan and find strategies to overcome the challenges. This approach helps them feel more in control and less overwhelmed by their emotions.

Encourage activities that promote emotional well-being, such as drawing, journaling, or engaging in hobbies they enjoy. These activities can help children process their emotions and find healthy outlets for their feelings. For example, they might draw about their feelings or write a journal entry to express their thoughts. These creative outlets provide a constructive way to deal with emotions and enhance their emotional intelligence.

By guiding your children in understanding and managing their emotions through a Christ-centered approach, you help them build resilience, empathy, and self-awareness. This foundation supports their overall emotional health and aligns their responses with their faith, fostering positive relationships and a balanced emotional life.

Teaching children to identify, express, and control their emotions.

Teaching children to identify, express, and control their emotions involves guiding them through a process of self-awareness, communication, and regulation. By providing them with practical tools and strategies, you help them develop emotional intelligence that aligns with Christian values.

Begin by helping your children recognize and name their emotions. Use simple language and age-appropriate activities to assist them in identifying how they feel. For younger children, you might use emotion cards with faces showing different feelings like happy, sad, or angry. Ask them to pick the card that best represents their current emotion. For older children, encourage them to describe their feelings using words and phrases. For example, if they are upset about a situation, ask them to explain why they feel that way and what they think might help improve their mood.

Teach your children how to express their emotions appropriately. Explain that it's important to communicate their feelings in a way that is respectful and constructive. Role-play different scenarios with them to practice expressing emotions clearly and calmly. For instance, if they are frustrated, guide them in using "I feel" statements like, "I feel frustrated when I can't understand my homework." This approach helps them communicate their feelings without placing blame or creating conflict.

Help your children understand that expressing their emotions is not just about saying how they feel but also about understanding why they feel that way. Encourage them to reflect on the reasons behind their emotions. For example, if they are feeling anxious, talk with them about what might be causing their anxiety and how they can address it. This reflective practice helps them connect their feelings to specific situations and gain insight into their emotional responses.

Introduce them to strategies for managing and controlling their emotions. Guide them in using methods like deep breathing, counting to ten, or taking a break to relax. For example, if they are angry, guide them in taking deep breaths to help them relax before responding. Explain that these techniques can help them manage their emotions in a way that aligns with their Christian values, such as responding with patience and kindness.

Encourage your children to use prayer as a tool for managing their emotions. Teach them that prayer can provide comfort and guidance when they are struggling with their feelings. For instance, if they are feeling overwhelmed, guide them in praying for peace and strength. Help them understand that prayer is a way to seek support and find reassurance in their faith.

Provide opportunities for your children to practice emotional regulation in real-life situations. For example, if they are having a disagreement with a sibling, guide them in using the skills they've learned to express their feelings and find a resolution. Encourage them to use their problem-solving skills to address conflicts in a way that is respectful and fair.

Reinforce the idea that controlling emotions involves making choices. Teach your children that they can choose how they respond to their feelings. For example, if they are feeling disappointed because they didn't win a game, help them see that they can choose to handle their disappointment gracefully rather than letting it affect their behavior. This perspective empowers them to take responsibility for their reactions and align them with their faith values.

Create a supportive environment where your children feel safe to explore and express their emotions. Let them know that it's okay to have a range of feelings and that they can always come to you for support. Regularly check in with them about how they're feeling and offer guidance as needed. This open communication helps them feel understood and valued, which is crucial for their emotional development.

Model emotional regulation in your own behavior. Show your children how you manage your own emotions and navigate challenging situations with composure and grace. Share with them how your faith helps you in these moments and discuss the biblical principles that guide your responses. For instance, you might talk about how trusting in God's plan helps you stay calm during stressful times.

By teaching your children to identify, express, and control their emotions, you equip them with essential skills for emotional well-being and personal growth. This guidance helps them navigate their feelings in a way that is aligned with Christian values, fostering a balanced and compassionate approach to their emotional lives.

Biblical principles for dealing with anger, fear, and sadness.

Biblical principles for dealing with anger, fear, and sadness provide guidance on how to manage these emotions in ways that reflect Christian values and teachings. By incorporating these principles, you help children learn to handle their feelings constructively and align their responses with their faith.

When addressing anger, the Bible offers several key teachings on how to manage this intense emotion. Proverbs 15:1 (KJV) states, "A soft answer turneth away wrath: but grievous words stir up anger." This verse highlights the importance of responding to anger with calmness and gentle words. Teach your children that when they feel angry, they should focus on using kind and measured language rather than reacting with harsh words or behavior. Encourage them to pause and take a moment to breathe or pray before responding in a situation where they feel anger rising.

Another relevant passage is Ephesians 4:26 (KJV), which says, "Be ye angry, and sin not: let not the sun go down upon your wrath." This verse emphasizes that feeling angry is not a sin, but it is important to address anger in a way that does not lead to sinful actions. Teach your children that it is okay to feel anger, but they should work to resolve the issue and seek reconciliation before the end of the day. Encourage them to communicate openly and seek forgiveness if their anger has caused harm to others.

For fear, the Bible provides reassurance that God is a source of comfort and strength. Isaiah 41:10 (KJV) assures us, "Fear thou not; for I am with thee: be not dismayed; for I am thy God: I will strengthen thee; yea, I will help thee; yea, I will uphold thee with the right hand of my righteousness." This verse reminds us that we do not face our fears alone; God is with us and will provide support. Teach your children to turn to God in prayer when they are feeling fearful, and remind them that they can seek comfort and strength from their faith.

Psalm 34:4 (KJV) also offers comfort for fear: "I sought the Lord, and he heard me, and delivered me from all my fears." Encourage your children to pray and seek God's guidance when they are afraid. Share stories from the Bible where characters faced fearful situations but found courage and support through their faith. This can help them understand that fear is a natural emotion, but their faith can provide them with courage and reassurance.

When dealing with sadness, the Bible offers encouragement and the promise of God's presence during difficult times. Psalm 34:18 (KJV) states, "The Lord is nigh unto them that are of a broken heart; and saveth such as be of a contrite spirit." This verse emphasizes that God is close to those who are experiencing sadness and suffering. Teach your children that it is okay to feel sad and that God is always near, ready to offer comfort and support.

Another passage, Matthew 5:4 (KJV), says, "Blessed are they that mourn: for they shall be comforted." This verse assures us that mourning and sadness are recognized, and comfort will come. Encourage your children to express their sadness and seek comfort from God. Remind them that they can find solace through prayer and in the support of their Christian community.

By teaching these biblical principles, you help your children understand that managing emotions such as anger, fear, and sadness involves turning to God for guidance and comfort. These teachings provide a framework for handling emotions in a way that aligns with their faith, fostering a sense of peace and resilience in the face of life's challenges.

Chapter 6
Positive Discipline and Grace

Discipline and punishment are terms that are often used interchangeably, but they have distinct meanings and implications, especially within the context of Christian parenting. Understanding the difference between discipline and punishment is crucial for fostering a positive and loving environment for children. Discipline is about teaching and guiding children, whereas punishment focuses on correcting behavior through consequences.

Discipline is rooted in the idea of nurturing and guiding children toward understanding and improving their behavior. It is a proactive approach that emphasizes teaching and modeling appropriate behavior. For example, if a child makes a mistake, discipline involves explaining why the behavior was incorrect and helping them learn how to make better choices in the future. It focuses on the child's growth and development, aiming to build character and understanding.

Punishment, on the other hand, is often reactive and aims to correct behavior through consequences. It is more about administering a penalty or inflicting a consequence for wrongdoing. While punishment can sometimes deter undesired behavior, it may not always lead to understanding or growth. For example, if a child is punished by losing privileges for a misstep, the focus might be more on the consequence rather than the learning experience that could lead to better behavior in the future.

In Christian parenting, the approach to discipline should align with biblical principles of love, grace, and forgiveness. Hebrews 12:6 (KJV) says, "For whom the Lord loveth he chasteneth, and scourgeth every son whom he receiveth." This verse reflects the idea that discipline, when done with love, is a form of care and guidance. It shows that discipline should not be about punishment but about guiding children in a way that reflects God's love and care for them.

Proverbs 13:24 (KJV) offers another perspective: "He that spareth his rod hateth his son: but he that loveth him chasteneth him betimes." This verse can be interpreted to mean that discipline is an expression of love and concern for a child's well-being. It suggests that discipline should be consistent and timely, aimed at helping the child learn and grow rather than simply punishing them for mistakes.

Effective discipline in a Christian home involves setting clear expectations and consistently reinforcing them with love and patience. It's important to communicate why certain behaviors are unacceptable and to provide guidance on how to make better choices. For example, if a child disobeys a rule, instead of focusing on the punishment, discuss why the rule is important and how following it benefits them and others. This helps the child understand the reasons behind the rules and encourages them to make positive decisions.

Incorporating grace into discipline means approaching the child with understanding and compassion. Just as God extends grace to us, we should extend grace to our children when they make mistakes. This involves recognizing that they are still learning and growing and that mistakes are a natural part of the process. When discipline is administered with grace, it helps children feel loved and supported rather than simply feeling punished.

Practical ways to apply positive discipline include using positive reinforcement to encourage desired behavior. Praise and rewards for good behavior help children understand what is expected and motivate them to repeat those behaviors. Additionally, having open and honest conversations with children about their actions and the consequences helps them develop a sense of responsibility and self-awareness.

It's also important to model appropriate behavior and handle conflicts with patience and understanding. Children learn a great deal from observing how their parents handle challenges and disagreements. By demonstrating calm and constructive ways to address issues, parents can teach their children how to manage their own behavior and emotions effectively.

Overall, positive discipline in a Christian home is about guiding children with love and grace, focusing on their growth and development rather than simply correcting their mistakes. By understanding the difference between discipline and punishment and applying biblical principles, parents can create a nurturing environment that helps children develop into compassionate, confident, and Christ-centered individuals.

Implementing grace-based discipline.

Implementing grace-based discipline involves applying principles of compassion, patience, and forgiveness in the way you guide your child's behavior. This approach emphasizes understanding and nurturing rather than simply enforcing rules and administering consequences. By focusing on grace, you create an environment where children feel supported in their growth and learning.

Start by setting clear, fair expectations for behavior. Clearly communicate the rules and the reasons behind them. Ensure your child understands what is expected and why these expectations are important. For example, if you set a rule about screen time, explain not only the limit but also why it's beneficial for their overall well-being and development. This helps them see the purpose behind the rules, making them more likely to respect and follow them.

When a child makes a mistake or breaks a rule, approach the situation with empathy and a desire to understand their perspective. Instead of reacting with immediate frustration or anger, take a moment to listen to their side of the story. Ask questions to understand their reasoning and feelings. For instance, if a child fails to complete their homework, discuss what challenges they faced rather than focusing solely on the missed assignment. This helps them feel heard and respected, and it opens the door to constructive conversations about solutions and improvements.

Apply correction with a focus on teaching and guiding rather than punishing. Use the opportunity to help your child learn from their mistake. For example, if a child is disruptive in a social setting, rather than simply reprimanding them, discuss with them why their behavior was inappropriate and what they can do differently in the future. Provide them with tools and strategies to handle similar situations better. This approach emphasizes growth and development rather than merely enforcing consequences.

Incorporate forgiveness and second chances into your discipline approach. Recognize that everyone, including children, makes mistakes and that these are opportunities for learning rather than occasions for harsh judgment. If a child apologizes and shows a willingness to make amends, acknowledge their effort and give them the chance to correct their behavior. For example, if a child argues with a sibling and later apologizes, reinforce their positive steps by discussing how they can resolve conflicts more effectively in the future. This encourages them to take responsibility for their actions while also feeling supported and valued.

Encourage positive behavior by reinforcing good actions with praise and rewards. Highlight and celebrate when your child makes positive choices or shows improvement. For instance, if they help with chores without being asked, offer specific praise and perhaps a small reward. This positive reinforcement helps them understand what behaviors are desirable and motivates them to continue making good choices.

Model grace-based behavior yourself. Children learn a great deal by observing their parents. Demonstrate patience, understanding, and forgiveness in your own interactions and responses. Show them how to handle mistakes and conflicts with grace and respect. For example, if you make an error or face a challenging situation, model how to address it calmly and constructively. Share with them how your faith guides your responses and decisions, helping them see how grace can be applied in everyday life.

Incorporate prayer and reflection into your discipline approach. Encourage your child to pray about their feelings and challenges, and pray together as a family when addressing behavioral issues. Use these moments to seek guidance from God on how to handle situations with grace and wisdom. Prayer can be a powerful tool for both you and your child to find peace and understanding in difficult moments.

Overall, grace-based discipline is about fostering a nurturing environment where children feel supported and understood as they learn and grow. By focusing on empathy, teaching, and forgiveness, you help them develop a strong moral foundation and emotional resilience. This approach aligns with Christian values and helps children build a positive relationship with both their faith and their family.

Balancing boundaries with unconditional love.

Balancing boundaries with unconditional love is essential in creating a nurturing and supportive environment for children. This balance helps children feel secure while also understanding the importance of rules and expectations. It combines the firmness of boundaries with the warmth and acceptance of unconditional love.

Start by establishing clear and consistent boundaries. Boundaries give structure and help children understand what's acceptable behavior. Clearly communicate these limits and the reasons behind them. For example, if you set a rule about bedtime, explain why it's important for their health and well-being. Consistent enforcement of boundaries helps children know what to expect and what is expected of them.

However, it's equally important to convey that these boundaries are rooted in love and concern for their well-being. Emphasize that rules are not meant to be restrictive but to guide them in making good choices. For instance, if a child struggles with curfew, explain that the rule is there to keep them safe and help them develop responsibility. This helps children understand that boundaries are not arbitrary but are intended to support their growth and safety.

Unconditional love means showing acceptance and affection regardless of behavior. Even when children make mistakes or break rules, let them know that your love for them is unwavering. For example, if a child forgets to complete their chores, address the issue calmly and remind them of the importance of the responsibility. At the same time, reassure them of your love and support. This helps them feel secure and valued, even when they face consequences.

Use moments of misbehavior as opportunities to reinforce both boundaries and love. When correcting behavior, approach the situation with empathy and understanding. Focus on the behavior rather than labeling the child. For example, if a child acts out, discuss the specific behavior that needs to change and why, rather than expressing disappointment in them as a person. This approach helps maintain their self-esteem while guiding them toward better choices.

Encourage open communication and allow children to express their feelings and perspectives. Listen to their concerns and validate their emotions, even if you need to enforce boundaries. For instance, if a child is upset about a restriction on screen time, acknowledge their feelings and explain the reasoning behind the limit. This helps them feel heard and respected while still adhering to the boundaries you've set.

Model the balance of boundaries and unconditional love in your own behavior. Demonstrate how to handle challenges and conflicts with respect and care. Show how you can be firm in your expectations while also expressing love and support. For example, if you are faced with a difficult situation at work or in your personal life, handle it with composure and discuss it openly with your child. This demonstrates how to navigate life's challenges while maintaining a loving and supportive approach.

Incorporate regular family discussions about values, expectations, and feelings. Use these discussions to reinforce the idea that boundaries are there to protect and guide, not to punish. Encourage your child to share their thoughts and questions about the rules and expectations. This creates an environment of mutual respect and understanding, where boundaries are seen as part of a loving and supportive relationship.

Balancing boundaries with unconditional love involves maintaining consistency in expectations while providing emotional support and affirmation. By clearly setting and enforcing boundaries with compassion, you help your child develop a sense of security and understanding. This balance fosters a positive and loving environment where children can thrive and feel valued, both for their behavior and their inherent worth.

Part 3

Building Confidence in Christ

Chapter 7
Encouraging God-Given Gifts and Talents

Encouraging God-given gifts and talents involves helping your children recognize and develop their unique abilities while grounding their growth in their faith. It's about creating an environment where they feel supported and inspired to explore their potential.

Start by observing your child's interests and strengths. Pay attention to what activities they enjoy and where they show natural abilities. For instance, if your child loves drawing and spends hours creating art, this might be a sign of a gift in creativity. If they excel in problem-solving and enjoy puzzles, they might have a talent for logical thinking. Recognizing these signs early can help you guide them in nurturing their talents.

Support their interests by providing opportunities to explore and develop their gifts. Enroll them in classes or activities related to their interests, such as art classes for a budding artist or a music group for a child with a passion for singing. Offer resources and tools that allow them to practice and enhance their skills. If your child is interested in sports, encourage them to join a team or take lessons to improve their abilities.

Encourage them by showing genuine interest and praise their efforts. Recognize and celebrate their achievements, no matter how minor, and acknowledge their progress. For example, if your child completes a painting or finishes a challenging project, commend their hard work and creativity. Positive reinforcement helps build their confidence and motivates them to continue pursuing their interests.

Help your child understand that their gifts are part of their unique identity and purpose. Teach them that their talents are a way to serve others and glorify God. Discuss how their abilities can be used to make a positive impact in their community or church. For instance, if your child is skilled in music, they might participate in church services or community events. This perspective helps them see their gifts as a way to fulfill a higher purpose and contribute to something greater than themselves.

Encourage a growth mindset by focusing on effort and persistence rather than just innate ability. Help your child understand that developing their talents requires hard work and dedication. For example, if they struggle with a particular skill, reassure them that it's normal to face challenges and that perseverance is key to improvement. Emphasize the importance of practice and learning from mistakes as part of their journey.

Involve faith in the process by integrating prayer and reflection into their development. Pray with your child about their talents and ask for guidance on how to use their gifts in alignment with God's will. Encourage them to seek God's direction and blessings as they pursue their interests. This spiritual aspect can provide them with a sense of purpose and motivation as they grow their abilities.

Offer chances for them to showcase their talents to others. Encourage them to participate in community service or church activities where they can use their gifts to benefit others. For example, if your child is skilled in baking, they might bake goods for a charity event or church gathering. Sharing their talents in this way helps them see the impact of their abilities and fosters a sense of generosity and service.

Model the value of using gifts and talents in your own life. Show how you use your abilities to serve others and follow your passions. Whether it's through your work, hobbies, or volunteer activities, demonstrate how you use your gifts in a way that aligns with your faith. This not only sets a positive example but also reinforces the idea that using one's talents is an important part of living a faith-driven life.

Encourage your child to set goals related to their talents and work towards them. Help them break down their goals into manageable steps and celebrate their achievements along the way. For instance, if their goal is to perform in a local concert, support their preparation and acknowledge their progress leading up to the event. This approach helps them stay motivated and focused on their personal development.

By creating an environment that nurtures and supports your child's God-given gifts, you help them build confidence in their abilities and recognize their potential. This encouragement, combined with a foundation in faith, helps them grow into individuals who are not only skilled and talented but also deeply aware of their purpose and contributions in the world.

Building self-confidence through faith and purpose.

Building self-confidence through faith and purpose involves helping your child understand their worth and potential through a Christian lens. This approach fosters a strong sense of identity and self-assurance that is rooted in their relationship with God and their unique purpose in life.

Start by affirming your child's value and worth in God's eyes. Remind them regularly that they are loved and cherished by God, regardless of their achievements or failures. Share Bible verses that speak to their inherent worth, such as Psalm 139:14 (KJV), which says, "I will praise thee; for I am fearfully and wonderfully made: marvelous are thy works; and that my soul knoweth right well." This helps them understand that their value is intrinsic and not dependent on external validation.

Encourage your child to see their talents and abilities as gifts from God. Teach them that their unique skills and interests are part of God's plan for their life. Help them connect their passions and talents to a greater purpose by discussing how they can use their gifts to serve others and contribute to their community. For instance, if your child is talented in writing, they might use their skills to create stories or articles that inspire and uplift others, demonstrating how their gifts have a meaningful impact.

Foster self-confidence by setting achievable goals and celebrating their accomplishments. Help your child set realistic and specific goals related to their talents and interests. Break these goals into smaller, manageable steps and guide them through the process. For example, if your child is learning a new musical instrument, celebrate each milestone they reach, such as mastering a song or improving their technique. This positive reinforcement builds their confidence and motivates them to continue working towards their goals.

Teach resilience by encouraging your child to view challenges and setbacks as opportunities for growth. Help them understand that failure and difficulties are a natural part of life and can be valuable learning experiences. Share stories from the Bible, such as Joseph's journey from being sold into slavery to becoming a leader in Egypt, to illustrate how perseverance and faith can lead to eventual success. Emphasize the importance of resilience and a positive attitude in overcoming obstacles and achieving their goals.

Promote a growth mindset by focusing on effort and perseverance rather than just innate ability. Encourage your child to embrace challenges and view them as opportunities to develop their skills and character. For example, if your child struggles with a difficult subject at school, help them understand that with practice and determination, they can improve. Praise their effort and progress rather than just their results, reinforcing the idea that growth and learning are continuous processes.

Help your child connect their self-confidence to their faith by incorporating prayer and reflection into their daily routine. Encourage them to pray about their goals, challenges, and desires, seeking God's guidance and strength. Teach them to rely on prayer and faith to boost their confidence and overcome self-doubt. For example, if your child feels anxious about a performance or presentation, guide them in praying for calmness and assurance, reinforcing their trust in God's support.

Encourage your child to take on new challenges and responsibilities that align with their interests and abilities. Providing them with opportunities to step outside their comfort zone helps build their confidence and fosters a sense of accomplishment. For instance, if your child is interested in leadership, encourage them to take on a role in a school club or church group. This experience helps them develop new skills and gain confidence in their abilities.

Model self-confidence and a positive attitude in your own life. Demonstrate how faith and purpose influence your actions and decisions. Share your own experiences of overcoming challenges and achieving goals with a faith-based perspective. Your example reinforces the importance of integrating faith and purpose into daily life and encourages your child to follow your lead.

By helping your child build self-confidence through faith and purpose, you create a supportive environment where they can develop a strong sense of identity and self-assurance. This approach not only empowers them to pursue their goals with confidence but also grounds their self-worth in their relationship with God and their understanding of their unique purpose in life.

Encouraging children to use their gifts to serve God and others.

Encouraging children to use their gifts to serve God and others helps them understand that their talents are not just for personal gain but are meant to make a positive impact in the world. This approach fosters a sense of purpose and responsibility, helping children see how their abilities can be a blessing to others and a way to honor God.

Start by helping your child recognize their gifts and talents as blessings from God. Explain that God has given everyone unique abilities and that these gifts are meant to be used for His glory and to help others. Use Bible verses to reinforce this idea, such as 1 Peter 4:10 (KJV), which says, "As every man hath received the gift, even so minister the same one to another, as good stewards of the manifold grace of God." This verse emphasizes that each gift is an opportunity to serve and bless others.

Encourage your child to identify how their gifts can be used to help those around them. Have conversations about their interests and passions, and discuss practical ways they can use their talents to serve others. For example, if your child is artistic, they might create cards or artwork to cheer up someone who is ill or to decorate their church's children's area. If they enjoy cooking, they might bake treats to share with a local shelter or community event. Helping your child connect their talents to acts of service makes their gifts more meaningful and impactful.

Provide opportunities for your child to use their gifts in community or church settings. Involve them in activities and programs where they can contribute their skills and talents. For instance, if your child loves music, encourage them to participate in the church choir or play an instrument during services. If they have a knack for organizing, they might help with planning events or activities for a church group. These experiences give your child a sense of purpose and allow them to see the positive effects of their contributions.

Teach your child the importance of serving with a humble and generous spirit. Emphasize that serving others is not about seeking recognition or praise but about showing love and kindness. Share examples from the Bible, such as the story of the Good Samaritan (Luke 10:25-37 KJV), to illustrate the value of serving others selflessly. Encourage your child to focus on the needs of others and to approach their service with a genuine desire to make a difference.

Help your child understand that their service to others is an expression of their faith and a way to honor God. Encourage them to pray about how they can use their gifts to serve and seek God's guidance in their efforts. Teach them to view their acts of service as a way to fulfill God's command to love and care for others. For example, if your child is volunteering at a community event, guide them in praying for the people they are serving and asking God to use their efforts to make a positive impact.

Celebrate and acknowledge your child's efforts and achievements in serving others. Recognize their contributions and express appreciation for their willingness to use their gifts for God's work. This positive reinforcement encourages them to continue using their talents in service and strengthens their commitment to making a difference. For instance, if your child helps with a charity fundraiser, praise their hard work and the difference they made, highlighting the value of their contributions.

Encourage your child to reflect on their experiences of serving others and to see how their gifts have made a difference. Have discussions about what they learned from their service and how it felt to use their talents for a greater purpose. This reflection helps them understand the impact of their actions and reinforces the importance of using their gifts to serve God and others.

By encouraging your child to use their gifts to serve God and others, you help them develop a sense of purpose and a deeper connection to their faith. This approach not only fosters a spirit of generosity and service but also helps children understand that their talents are a way to contribute to God's work and make a positive impact in the world.

Chapter 8
Overcoming Fear and Anxiety through Faith

Addressing fears and anxieties in children through faith involves understanding their concerns and guiding them with spiritual support and practical strategies. Children often experience fears about various aspects of their lives, such as school, social situations, or even safety. These fears can feel overwhelming and impact their daily lives. As a parent, helping your child navigate these emotions with faith can provide them with comfort and resilience.

Start by acknowledging your child's fears and anxieties without dismissing them. Let them know that it's okay to feel scared or worried and that their feelings are valid. Show empathy and patience as they express their concerns. For instance, if a child is anxious about starting a new school, listen to their worries and reassure them that it's normal to feel nervous about new experiences. This approach helps build trust and opens the door for further guidance.

Incorporate prayer into your routine as a way to address fears. Encourage your child to pray about their anxieties and seek God's peace and guidance. Prayer can be a powerful tool for calming the mind and heart. Teach your child simple prayers that ask for God's help in overcoming their fears. For example, a prayer might be, "Dear God, I am feeling scared about [specific situation]. Please help me to be brave and know that You are with me." This practice helps children turn to faith as a source of comfort.

Introduce Bible verses that speak to overcoming fear and finding peace. Verses like Philippians 4:6-7 (KJV) offer reassurance, saying, "Be careful for nothing; but in every thing by prayer and supplication with thanksgiving let your requests be made known unto God. And the peace of God, which passeth all understanding, shall keep your hearts and minds through Christ Jesus." Share these verses with your child and discuss their meanings. Encourage your child to memorize or write down verses that resonate with them, creating a personal resource for times of anxiety.

Teach your child to use their faith to confront fears. Help them understand that God is always with them, even in challenging situations. Explain that faith in God can provide strength and courage. For example, when facing a fear of the dark, remind them that God's presence is a constant source of light and protection. Use stories from the Bible where individuals faced fears with faith, such as David and Goliath or Daniel in the lion's den. These stories can illustrate how faith helped others overcome their fears.

Provide practical strategies to manage anxiety. Encourage your child to practice deep breathing exercises, engage in calming activities, or use relaxation techniques when they feel anxious. Help them create a comfort kit with items that help them feel secure, like a favorite book, a comforting toy, or a photo of family. These tools can offer immediate relief and help them feel more in control.

Model calmness and confidence when addressing fears. Children often take cues from their parents on how to handle stress and anxiety. Show them how you manage your own worries with faith and practical steps. For example, if you're dealing with a stressful situation, talk about how you're praying and trusting in God's plan. This modeling helps children learn to apply similar strategies in their own lives.

Encourage open communication about fears. Create a safe space where your child feels comfortable discussing their anxieties. Regularly check in with them about their feelings and offer support and encouragement. This ongoing dialogue helps children feel understood and supported, reducing the impact of their fears.

Involve your child in faith-based activities that promote confidence and peace. Activities such as attending church, participating in youth groups, or engaging in service projects can help children build a sense of community and support. These experiences reinforce their faith and provide positive outlets for managing anxiety.

Finally, celebrate and acknowledge your child's progress in overcoming fears. Praise their efforts and resilience as they use their faith and practical strategies to handle anxieties. Recognize their achievements, no matter how small, and encourage them to continue applying their faith in challenging situations. This positive reinforcement builds their confidence and reinforces the effectiveness of their faith-based approach to overcoming fear.

Teaching children to rely on God in difficult times.

Teaching children to rely on God during difficult times is essential in nurturing their spiritual resilience and trust. When challenges arise, children can benefit greatly from understanding that God is a steadfast source of strength and comfort.

Begin by explaining to your child that everyone faces difficult times, and it's natural to feel overwhelmed or unsure. Reassure them that it's okay to have these feelings and that turning to God can provide support and guidance. Use simple language to make these concepts accessible, such as saying, "When we face tough times, God is like a loving friend who helps us through."

Incorporate Bible stories that demonstrate God's support during hardships. For example, the story of Joseph in Egypt shows how God was with him through betrayal and imprisonment, ultimately leading him to a position where he could help others. Share these stories with your child, emphasizing how God was present in each situation and how faith helped the individuals involved.

Encourage your child to develop a habit of prayer as a means of seeking God's help. Teach them how to pray about their worries and struggles, guiding them to express their feelings honestly and ask for God's assistance. For example, a child might pray, "Dear God, I am feeling scared about [specific problem]. Please help me to feel brave and trust that You are with me." Reassure them that God listens to their prayers and cares about their concerns.

Introduce them to scripture that speaks to God's presence in times of trouble. Verses like Psalm 46:1 (KJV) state, "God is our refuge and strength, a very present help in trouble." Reading and discussing such verses can help children understand that God is always there to support them. Encourage them to memorize verses that resonate with them and keep these scriptures in mind during tough times.

Model reliance on God in your own life. Children learn by observing their parents, so demonstrate how you turn to God during your own challenges. Share age-appropriate stories about times when your faith helped you through difficulties. For instance, you might explain how prayer and trust in God helped you deal with a stressful situation at work or a personal challenge.

Teach your child practical ways to rely on God. Encourage them to create a "faith toolkit" that includes prayers, Bible verses, or comforting rituals. For instance, they might write down their worries and pray over them or keep a journal of God's blessings and answered prayers. These tools provide tangible ways for children to connect with their faith during hard times.

Create a supportive environment at home where children feel safe discussing their fears and challenges. Let them know that they can always talk to you about what's troubling them and that together you can pray for guidance and strength. This open communication helps them feel secure and supported in their reliance on God.

Encourage participation in faith-based activities that reinforce trust in God. Activities such as church services, youth groups, or faith-based community projects can provide additional support and foster a sense of belonging. These experiences remind children that they are part of a larger faith community that supports and uplifts them.

Lastly, celebrate moments when your child successfully relies on God to navigate a challenge. Recognize their efforts and progress, no matter how small, and offer praise for their trust and faith. This positive reinforcement builds their confidence and strengthens their belief in God's support.

Biblical verses and prayers for comfort and courage.

When guiding children through challenging moments, Biblical verses and prayers can offer significant comfort and courage. These spiritual resources help them connect with their faith and find solace in God's promises.

Start by introducing your child to a selection of comforting Bible verses. Choose passages that are simple and easy for them to understand. For instance, Psalm 34:4 (KJV) says, "I sought the Lord, and he heard me, and delivered me from all my fears." Explain that this verse assures them that God listens to their prayers and helps them through their fears.

Another reassuring verse is Isaiah 41:10 (KJV): "Fear thou not; for I am with thee: be not dismayed; for I am thy God: I will strengthen thee; yea, I will help thee; yea, I will uphold thee with the right hand of my righteousness." This passage emphasizes that God is always with them, providing strength and support.

Encourage your child to memorize these verses. Repetition helps embed these promises in their hearts, making them accessible during stressful times. You might create a memory verse chart together, decorating it with illustrations or stickers to make the process enjoyable and engaging.

Next, teach your child to use prayers as a way to seek comfort and courage. Begin with simple prayers that reflect their concerns and needs. For example, a comforting prayer might be, "Dear God, I am feeling scared and worried right now. Please help me feel your presence and give me the courage to face this challenge. Amen." This prayer focuses on asking for God's presence and courage, aligning with their immediate needs.

Guide your child in creating their own prayers. Encourage them to speak honestly about their feelings and ask God for specific help. For instance, they might pray, "God, I'm nervous about my big test tomorrow. Please help me stay calm and remember what I've learned. Thank you for always being with me." Personal prayers make the experience more meaningful and relatable.

Incorporate prayers of thanksgiving and praise into their routine. Teach them to thank God for His guidance and blessings even during tough times. A prayer of gratitude might be, "Thank you, God, for helping me through today. I appreciate your love and support. Please continue to guide me and help me trust in you."

Encourage your child to keep a prayer journal where they can write or draw their concerns, prayers, and the ways they see God's answers. This practice not only helps them articulate their thoughts but also reflects on how God has provided comfort and courage.

For daily inspiration, use a verse or a prayer during mealtimes or bedtime. This regular incorporation of scripture and prayer helps reinforce their importance and provides a comforting routine. For example, you might end the day with a simple prayer like, "Lord, thank you for today. Help me to trust you and find peace in your presence as I sleep. Amen."

As you share these Biblical verses and prayers, remind your child that these resources are not just for moments of fear or anxiety but are also a way to maintain a close relationship with God. Reiterate that God's promises are a constant source of strength and comfort, available to them at any time.

Chapter 9
Developing a Strong Moral Compass

Instilling Christian values and ethics in your children helps them navigate the world with a sense of purpose and integrity. A strong moral compass is essential for making choices that reflect their faith and build character. Here's how to nurture these values effectively.

Begin by setting a clear example. Live out the Christian values you wish to instill in them. Demonstrate kindness, honesty, and respect in your daily interactions. Show them how you handle situations with integrity and faith. When they see you making decisions based on Christian principles, they are more likely to adopt these values themselves.

Teach them about Biblical values and stories. Use age-appropriate Bible stories to illustrate moral lessons. For instance, the story of the Good Samaritan (Luke 10:25-37, KJV) teaches compassion and kindness. Discuss these stories with your children, focusing on the lessons they impart about treating others with love and respect.

Incorporate Christian ethics into everyday discussions. Talk openly about what it means to live a Christ-centered life. Discuss concepts like honesty, forgiveness, and humility regularly. For example, if a child faces a situation where they might be tempted to lie, use it as an opportunity to discuss the value of truthfulness. Explain how honesty honors God and builds trust with others.

Encourage reflection and self-examination. Help your children understand the importance of reflecting on their actions and decisions. Teach them to ask themselves if their choices align with their Christian values. Encourage them to pray for guidance when they face difficult decisions. This practice helps them develop a personal connection to their moral compass and understand its importance in their daily lives.

Involve them in service activities. Participate in community service or church activities as a family. This not only reinforces the importance of helping others but also provides practical experience in living out Christian values. Whether it's volunteering at a local shelter or helping a neighbor, these activities teach children about compassion and the joy of serving others.

Create a family mission statement. Develop a statement that reflects your family's Christian values and goals. This can serve as a guide for making decisions and resolving conflicts. Share this mission statement with your children and discuss how it aligns with your faith and values. Regularly revisit and discuss this statement to keep it relevant and meaningful.

Use everyday situations as teaching moments. When issues arise, use them to discuss Christian ethics and values. If a child is upset with a friend, talk about forgiveness and the importance of mending relationships. If they witness an injustice, discuss how they can respond with compassion and fairness. These conversations help them apply Christian principles in real-life scenarios.

Encourage moral courage. Teach your children the importance of standing up for what is right, even when it's difficult. Share stories of Biblical figures who demonstrated courage in their faith, such as Daniel in the lion's den (Daniel 6, KJV). Help them understand that being a Christian sometimes means making tough choices and standing firm in their beliefs.

Foster an environment of open communication. Create a space where your children feel comfortable discussing their thoughts and struggles. Encourage them to talk about their values and how they can apply them in their lives. Listen to their concerns and provide guidance that aligns with Christian teachings.

Praise their efforts to live out Christian values. Recognize and affirm their attempts to make ethical decisions and show compassion. Positive reinforcement helps them see the value in living a Christ-centered life and motivates them to continue growing in their faith.

Guiding children to make decisions based on their faith.

Helping children make decisions based on their faith involves guiding them through the process of considering Christian values and teachings when faced with choices. Here's a comprehensive approach to support them in integrating their beliefs into their decision-making.

Start by teaching them the importance of prayer in decision-making. Encourage your children to pray before making important decisions. Explain that prayer helps them seek God's guidance and wisdom. Create a routine where they can express their concerns and ask for God's direction. This practice reinforces their reliance on God and fosters a habit of seeking divine input in their choices.

Introduce them to Biblical principles that can guide their decisions. Share relevant scriptures that offer wisdom on various aspects of life. For example, Proverbs 3:5-6 (KJV) teaches the importance of trusting in the Lord and seeking His guidance. Help them understand how these principles apply to everyday situations, such as choosing friends, handling conflicts, or making academic decisions.

Encourage them to consider the impact of their decisions on others. Teach them to think about how their choices affect those around them. Use Biblical examples, like the story of Joseph, who, despite being wronged by his brothers, chose forgiveness and integrity (Genesis 37-50, KJV). Discuss how acting with love and respect aligns with Christian teachings and benefits others.

Help them evaluate their options through the lens of Christian values. When faced with a decision, guide them in considering which option best reflects their faith. Ask questions that prompt them to think about honesty, kindness, and justice. For instance, if they are deciding whether to help a classmate, discuss how their choice aligns with the Christian value of serving others.

Teach them to seek counsel from trusted Christian adults. Encourage them to talk to you, other family members, or church leaders when they face difficult decisions. Explain that seeking advice from those who share their faith can provide valuable perspectives and support. It also helps them learn to rely on a community of faith for guidance.

Encourage reflection on past decisions. Discuss previous choices they've made and the outcomes of those decisions. Reflect on how their faith influenced their choices and what they learned from the experience. This reflection helps them see the practical benefits of making decisions based on their Christian beliefs and encourages growth in their decision-making skills.

Promote accountability and responsibility. Help your children understand the importance of taking responsibility for their decisions, whether the outcomes are positive or negative. Discuss how to handle mistakes with grace and learn from them, using Biblical examples of repentance and growth, like King David's story (2 Samuel 11-12, KJV).

Model decision-making based on faith. Share your own decision-making process with them. Explain how you consider Biblical teachings and pray for guidance when making choices. This not only provides them with a practical example but also helps them see the relevance of faith in everyday life.

Encourage them to write down their decisions and the reasons behind them. This practice can help them clarify their thoughts and see how their faith influenced their choices. Reviewing these notes periodically can also help them recognize patterns in their decision-making and grow in their understanding of how faith guides their actions.

Foster a supportive environment for decision-making. Create a safe space where your children feel comfortable discussing their choices and seeking advice. Offer encouragement and support as they navigate their decisions, reinforcing that their faith is a valuable tool for making wise and ethical choices.

The importance of integrity and honesty in a Christ-centered life.

Integrity and honesty are fundamental to living a Christ-centered life. They are key aspects of character that reflect one's commitment to Christian values and teachings. Understanding their importance helps children develop strong moral principles that guide their actions and interactions with others.

Integrity involves being consistent in actions, values, and beliefs. It means doing the right thing even when no one is watching. In the context of a Christ-centered life, integrity reflects a commitment to living according to God's commandments and teachings. For instance, Proverbs 11:3 (KJV) states, "The integrity of the upright shall guide them: but the perverseness of transgressors shall destroy them." This verse emphasizes that living with integrity provides guidance and leads to a righteous path.

Honesty is another vital aspect of a Christ-centered life. It means being truthful in words and actions. Honesty builds trust and demonstrates respect for others. Ephesians 4:25 (KJV) teaches, "Wherefore putting away lying, speak every man truth with his neighbour: for we are members one of another." This scripture highlights the importance of truthfulness in maintaining healthy relationships and fostering a sense of community.

Incorporating integrity and honesty into daily life involves several practical steps. First, it is essential to model these values in everyday actions. Children learn by observing, so demonstrating honesty and integrity in your own life provides a clear example for them to follow. For example, being truthful in your dealings with others, honoring commitments, and admitting mistakes are all ways to showcase these values.

Second, create opportunities for discussions about integrity and honesty. Engage your children in conversations about why these values matter and how they impact their lives and relationships. Use Biblical stories and examples to illustrate the importance of living with integrity. The story of Daniel in the lion's den (Daniel 6, KJV) is a powerful example of standing firm in one's principles despite facing adversity.

Encourage your children to reflect on their own actions and decisions. Help them recognize situations where integrity and honesty are tested. Discuss how they can apply Christian teachings to these situations. For instance, if they face a dilemma at school or with friends, guide them through the process of making choices that align with their faith and values.

Teach them the benefits of living with integrity and honesty. Explain how these values lead to strong relationships, self-respect, and a clear conscience. Highlight that integrity and honesty build trust with others and bring a sense of peace and fulfillment that comes from living authentically.

Address the challenges of maintaining integrity and honesty. Acknowledge that it can be difficult to uphold these values, especially in situations where there is pressure to conform or when facing personal gain. Discuss strategies for overcoming these challenges, such as seeking God's strength through prayer, relying on Biblical guidance, and finding support from trusted mentors or community members.

Promote the practice of accountability. Encourage your children to hold themselves accountable for their actions and decisions. Teach them the importance of acknowledging mistakes, seeking forgiveness, and making amends. This practice reinforces the value of honesty and demonstrates a commitment to personal growth and integrity.

Reinforce the connection between integrity, honesty, and faith. Help your children understand that living a Christ-centered life means aligning their actions with God's teachings. By valuing integrity and honesty, they honor their relationship with God and reflect His character in their interactions with others.

Part 4

Maintaining a Strong Family Bond in Christ

Chapter 10
Strengthening Family Relationships

Fostering open communication and trust within the family is essential for strengthening relationships and creating a supportive, Christ-centered home environment. Effective communication and trust are the cornerstones of a healthy family dynamic, and they play a crucial role in nurturing strong bonds among family members.

To build open communication, start by creating an atmosphere where everyone feels safe to express their thoughts and feelings. This involves actively listening to each other without judgment. When family members know they will be heard, they are more likely to share openly. Encourage regular family meetings or discussions where everyone has a chance to speak. For instance, setting aside a time each week for a family meal or a discussion can help create a routine for sharing.

Modeling open communication is equally important. Children learn by observing their parents, so demonstrate how to communicate effectively by being honest and respectful in your interactions. Show that it's okay to discuss feelings, ask questions, and seek solutions together. For example, if a disagreement arises, handle it calmly and constructively, showing how to address issues without conflict.

Trust is built through consistency and reliability. When family members know they can depend on each other, trust grows. Keep your promises and be consistent in your actions. If you commit to something, follow through. This reliability shows that you value and respect each family member's needs and expectations.

Transparency is another key element in building trust. Be open about your own thoughts and feelings, and encourage others to do the same. This openness helps avoid misunderstandings and builds a deeper connection between family members. For example, if you're feeling stressed or worried, share this with your family in an age-appropriate way, and discuss how you can support each other.

Encouraging empathy and understanding is crucial for maintaining strong family relationships. Teach your children to recognize and respect each other's emotions. Help them understand that everyone has their own perspective and feelings, and that it's important to be considerate of others' viewpoints. Practicing empathy fosters a supportive environment where everyone feels valued.

Set aside quality time to spend together as a family. Engaging in shared activities strengthens bonds and provides opportunities for meaningful conversations. Whether it's playing games, going on outings, or participating in family traditions, these experiences create lasting memories and reinforce the family connection.

Address conflicts and issues promptly and fairly. Avoid letting problems fester, as unresolved issues can erode trust and communication. When conflicts arise, approach them with a mindset of seeking solutions rather than placing blame. Encourage problem-solving together, and emphasize the importance of forgiveness and reconciliation.

Pray together as a family. Incorporating prayer into your daily routine can strengthen your spiritual connection and support open communication. Praying for each other's needs and concerns helps build a sense of unity and trust. It also provides an opportunity to reflect on your faith and seek guidance together.

Encourage positive reinforcement and affirmation. Recognize and celebrate each family member's achievements and efforts. Offering praise and encouragement builds self-esteem and reinforces a positive, trusting atmosphere. Simple acts of appreciation, like verbal affirmations or small gestures of kindness, go a long way in fostering a supportive family environment.

Promote a culture of mutual respect. Teach your children the importance of respecting each other's opinions and differences. Respect is fundamental to effective communication and trust. Encourage respectful interactions and address any disrespectful behavior promptly.

Support each other's personal growth and development. Show interest in each other's hobbies, goals, and aspirations. Providing encouragement and support for individual pursuits strengthens the family bond and demonstrates care for each other's well-being.

The role of forgiveness and reconciliation in the home.

Forgiveness and reconciliation are essential for keeping family harmony and strengthening relationships. These principles reflect the heart of Christian values and play a crucial role in creating a loving, supportive home environment. Understanding and practicing forgiveness and reconciliation helps to resolve conflicts, heal wounds, and build stronger, more resilient family bonds.

Forgiveness starts with recognizing that everyone makes mistakes. No one is perfect, and understanding this helps to foster a more compassionate and forgiving atmosphere. When family members wrong each other, it's essential to address the issue with a spirit of forgiveness rather than holding onto grudges or resentment.

Teach your children about the importance of forgiveness through your actions and words. Demonstrate how to forgive by letting go of past grievances and focusing on positive interactions. For instance, if a disagreement occurs, show how to resolve it by acknowledging mistakes, apologizing sincerely, and moving forward with a renewed understanding. Explain to your children that forgiveness is not just about forgetting but about choosing to let go of negative feelings and striving for a more harmonious relationship.

Encourage open conversations about feelings and grievances. Create a safe space where family members can express their emotions and discuss conflicts openly. This approach helps to address issues before they escalate and promotes a culture of understanding and empathy. When family members are encouraged to talk about their feelings, it becomes easier to work through problems and find common ground.

Reconciliation involves repairing relationships and restoring trust after a conflict or misunderstanding. It's about coming together and finding a way to move forward. Reconciliation requires humility, patience, and a willingness to listen and understand each other's perspectives. Encourage your family to approach reconciliation with a genuine desire to heal and rebuild relationships.

Model reconciliation by demonstrating how to resolve conflicts constructively. For example, if you and your spouse have a disagreement, show how to work through it by communicating openly, acknowledging each other's viewpoints, and finding a compromise. When children see this process in action, they learn valuable skills for managing their own conflicts and relationships.

Use Biblical teachings as a guide for forgiveness and reconciliation. The Bible offers many examples of forgiveness, such as the parable of the Prodigal Son, which illustrates the joy of reconciliation and the importance of forgiving others. Teach your children about these Biblical stories and encourage them to apply these lessons in their own lives.

Incorporate prayer into the process of forgiveness and reconciliation. Praying together as a family helps to seek God's guidance and strength in resolving conflicts. Ask for God's help in healing relationships and providing the grace to forgive. Prayer also serves as a reminder of the importance of maintaining a loving and forgiving heart.

Encourage acts of kindness and gestures of goodwill as part of the reconciliation process. Simple acts of kindness, such as writing a heartfelt note or offering a sincere apology, can help mend relationships and show a genuine commitment to repairing any damage. These actions reinforce the message that reconciliation involves not just words but also meaningful efforts to restore trust and connection.

Establishing family rituals or traditions that promote forgiveness and reconciliation can also be beneficial. For example, creating a family "gratitude jar" where each member can write down positive things about each other can help reinforce a culture of appreciation and understanding. These rituals serve as reminders of the importance of maintaining positive relationships and working through conflicts with a spirit of love and forgiveness.

Family activities that reinforce Christian values.

Family activities that reinforce Christian values help to create a strong, faith-centered environment where values like love, kindness, and service are practiced regularly. These activities offer practical ways to integrate faith into daily life, making Christian teachings more tangible and meaningful for all family members.

Plan family service projects as a way to put faith into action. Engaging in activities that benefit others, such as volunteering at a local food bank, participating in community clean-ups, or supporting charitable organizations, helps to teach the value of serving others. Choose projects that align with your family's interests and abilities, ensuring that everyone can contribute in a meaningful way. Discuss the impact of these activities and how they reflect Christian values of compassion and generosity.

Incorporate Christian-themed crafts and activities that reinforce biblical stories and teachings. For example, creating a "gratitude tree" where family members write down things they are thankful for on paper leaves and hang them on a tree, can be a visual reminder of God's blessings. Crafting Bible verse bookmarks or decorating a "prayer jar" where each member adds written prayers can also serve as tools for spiritual growth and reflection.

Celebrate Christian holidays and traditions with special family events that emphasize their spiritual significance. For Christmas, you might have a tradition of reading the Nativity story and singing carols that reflect the true meaning of the season. For Easter, consider a family discussion or activity focused on the resurrection of Jesus and the hope it brings. These celebrations not only reinforce Christian values but also create lasting memories and traditions centered around faith.

Encourage family discussions about moral and ethical dilemmas using Christian teachings as a guide. Discuss scenarios or current events in light of biblical principles and explore how to apply Christian values in everyday decisions. This practice helps to develop critical thinking skills while grounding your family's decisions in faith-based perspectives.

Create a family mission statement that reflects your Christian values and goals. Involve each family member in crafting a statement that emphasizes your collective commitment to living out Christian principles. Display this mission statement in a prominent place in your home as a constant reminder of your family's shared values and purpose.

Share and discuss Christian books, movies, and music that highlight values like love, faith, and forgiveness. Choose materials that are appropriate for the ages of your children and use them as a springboard for discussions about how these values can be applied in daily life. Watching a movie with a Christian theme or reading a book together provides a shared experience that can lead to meaningful conversations and reflections.

Lastly, foster a culture of gratitude and praise within your family. Make it a practice to regularly express thanks to God for His blessings and to celebrate the positive aspects of each day. This focus on gratitude helps to cultivate a positive outlook and reinforces the Christian value of recognizing and appreciating God's goodness.

Chapter 11
The Power of Prayer in Parenting

Praying for your children and with your children is a powerful way to support their spiritual growth and strengthen your family bond. It creates a foundation of faith and trust, showing them that they are cared for and that God is a constant presence in their lives.

Start by establishing a routine for praying for your children. Make it a regular part of your daily or weekly schedule. Find a quiet moment each day, perhaps during your own personal prayer time, to lift your children up in prayer. This can be as simple as asking for God's protection, guidance, and blessings for them. By consistently bringing them before God, you show your commitment to their well-being and spiritual development.

Be specific in your prayers. Rather than general prayers, focus on specific aspects of their lives—such as their schoolwork, friendships, and personal challenges. Pray for their strengths and weaknesses, asking God to help them grow in areas where they need support. For example, if your child is struggling with a particular subject in school, pray for their understanding and perseverance. If they're facing social difficulties, pray for their courage and kindness. This targeted approach makes your prayers more meaningful and demonstrates your attentiveness to their needs.

Encourage your children to be involved in praying with you. Set aside time for family prayer sessions where everyone participates. This practice can be integrated into daily routines, such as at mealtimes or bedtime, or during special moments like family gatherings. When praying together, involve your children by letting them voice their own prayers or express their concerns and gratitude. This not only helps them practice their own prayers but also deepens their connection to the faith.

Model sincere and heartfelt prayers. Show your children how to approach God with honesty and openness. Share your own prayers and discuss the things you're praying about, including any personal struggles or joys. By doing this, you help them understand that prayer is not just about asking for things but about building a relationship with God and seeking His presence in all aspects of life.

Encourage your children to pray for others as well. Teach them to include family members, friends, and those in need in their prayers. This practice fosters empathy and a sense of responsibility, aligning with the Christian values of love and service. It also helps them understand the broader impact of prayer and its role in supporting and uplifting others.

Pray with your children during challenging times. When they face difficulties, such as illness, family issues, or personal struggles, come together to pray for strength and comfort. This collective prayer time helps them feel supported and reassured, knowing that they are not alone in their struggles. It also reinforces the idea that God is a source of comfort and strength during difficult moments.

Make prayers for your children a part of special occasions and milestones. Whether it's celebrating a birthday, starting a new school year, or facing a significant life change, use these moments to pray for God's guidance and blessings. This practice highlights the importance of inviting God into all aspects of life and recognizing His role in their growth and achievements.

Teach your children to pray for their own needs and desires. Encourage them to express their thoughts and feelings to God, helping them understand that they can turn to Him with anything that concerns them. Offer guidance on how to frame their prayers, focusing on gratitude, requests, and seeking God's will. By doing so, you empower them to take an active role in their spiritual journey and build confidence in their ability to communicate with God.

Provide support and encouragement as they develop their prayer life. Celebrate their efforts and progress, and offer guidance when they face challenges in their prayers. This encouragement helps to build their confidence and reinforces the value of maintaining a consistent prayer practice.

Chapter 12
Navigating Modern Challenges with Faith

Navigating modern challenges with faith involves addressing contemporary issues such as technology, peer pressure, and secular influences in a way that aligns with Christian values. As parents, it is essential to guide children through these challenges by integrating faith into every aspect of their lives.

Technology plays a significant role in today's world, shaping how children learn, communicate, and interact. While technology offers many benefits, it also presents challenges. It is crucial to help children use technology in ways that support their faith and well-being. Start by setting clear boundaries on technology use. Create family rules about screen time, such as limiting time spent on devices and ensuring that technology is used for educational or constructive purposes. Encourage your children to engage in activities that promote their spiritual growth, such as listening to Christian music, watching faith-based programs, or using apps designed to support their faith journey.

It's also important to have open conversations about online behavior. Teach your children about the impact of their digital footprint and the importance of maintaining integrity and kindness in their online interactions. Discuss the potential dangers of the internet, such as cyberbullying, inappropriate content, and online predators. Equip them with strategies to handle these situations, and emphasize the importance of coming to you with any concerns or problems they encounter online.

Peer pressure is another challenge that many children face. Friends and social circles can strongly influence a child's choices and behaviors. To navigate this, help your children develop a strong sense of identity rooted in their faith. Reinforce the values and principles of Christianity, and encourage them to make decisions based on their beliefs rather than merely seeking approval from peers. Role-playing different scenarios can be a helpful way to prepare them for situations where they might face peer pressure.

Support your children in finding friends who share their values. Encourage participation in church groups, youth activities, and community service projects where they can meet like-minded individuals. Having a supportive network of friends who understand and respect their faith can make it easier for them to stand firm in their beliefs.

Secular influences can be pervasive in modern culture, often promoting values and behaviors that contradict Christian teachings. To address these influences, it's important to provide a strong counter-narrative at home. Foster an environment where Christian values are lived out and discussed regularly. Share Bible stories and teachings that relate to current issues and help your children understand how to apply their faith in everyday situations.

Encourage critical thinking and open dialogue about what they encounter in secular media. Discuss how certain messages or trends may conflict with Christian values and how they can discern and respond to these influences. By developing a thoughtful and informed approach to secular content, children can better navigate and resist negative influences.

Involving Faith in Everyday Life is key to overcoming modern challenges. Incorporate Christian practices into daily routines, such as prayer, Bible study, and attending church services. Make faith a natural part of discussions and decisions. By demonstrating how faith informs your own choices and actions, you model for your children how to integrate their beliefs into all aspects of life.

Building Resilience is another critical aspect of addressing modern challenges. Teach your children to rely on their faith for strength and guidance when facing difficulties. Encourage them to see challenges as opportunities for growth and learning. Remind them of Biblical promises and teachings that offer comfort and encouragement in tough times.

Family Activities can also play a role in strengthening faith and resilience. Engage in activities that reinforce Christian values, such as volunteering together, participating in church events, or studying the Bible as a family. These activities not only strengthen family bonds but also provide practical ways to apply faith to everyday situations.

Equipping children to stand firm in their faith in a changing world.

Equipping children to stand firm in their faith in a changing world involves preparing them to maintain their Christian values and beliefs despite the ever-evolving cultural and social landscape. This preparation is crucial for helping them navigate a world that often challenges their faith and offers conflicting messages.

Start by building a strong spiritual foundation. Ensure that your children have a solid understanding of Christian teachings and how these principles apply to their lives. Regular Bible study and discussions about faith can help them develop a deep-rooted belief system that is less likely to be swayed by external influences. Teach them about the core tenets of Christianity and the importance of living according to these values.

Encourage critical thinking and discerning judgment. Help your children analyze and evaluate the messages they encounter in the media, at school, and among their peers. Discuss various viewpoints and compare them with Christian teachings. This practice will help them develop the ability to critically assess information and make decisions that align with their faith.

Modeling faith in action is another vital aspect. Demonstrate how to live out Christian values in your daily life. Show them how you handle challenges, make ethical decisions, and interact with others in a Christ-like manner. By seeing these principles in practice, children learn to incorporate them into their own lives.

Provide a supportive community. Encourage your children to be part of a faith-based community where they can build relationships with others who share their beliefs. This support network can offer encouragement, guidance, and accountability, helping them remain steadfast in their faith. Engage them in church activities, youth groups, and service projects where they can connect with peers who reinforce their values.

Teach resilience and perseverance. Equip your children with strategies for dealing with opposition or criticism of their faith. Teach them how to respond with grace and confidence when their beliefs are challenged. Role-play different scenarios where they might encounter doubts or negative feedback and discuss how they can address these situations while remaining true to their faith.

Instill a sense of purpose by helping your children understand the role of their faith in their personal goals and aspirations. Encourage them to see their faith as a source of strength and guidance in pursuing their dreams and making decisions about their future. By linking their faith to their personal ambitions, they will be more motivated to uphold their beliefs in various aspects of their lives.

Encourage open dialogue about faith and its challenges. Create a safe environment where your children feel comfortable discussing their doubts, questions, and experiences related to their faith. By addressing these topics openly and honestly, you can help them navigate the complexities of their beliefs and reinforce their commitment to their Christian values.

Prepare them for cultural changes by discussing current events, trends, and societal shifts in the context of Christian teachings. Help them understand how to respond to these changes in a way that aligns with their faith. This proactive approach will enable them to face new challenges with confidence and clarity.

Pray with and for your children regularly, asking for God's guidance and strength to help them stand firm in their faith. Encourage them to develop their own prayer life and seek God's support in times of uncertainty or difficulty. Prayer can be a powerful tool for reinforcing their faith and providing comfort and direction in a changing world.

By combining these approaches, you can help your children develop the resilience, confidence, and understanding needed to navigate a complex and often challenging world while staying true to their Christian beliefs. This preparation will empower them to face various influences and pressures with a strong sense of purpose and unwavering faith.

Balancing Christian values with the realities of modern life.

Balancing Christian values with the realities of modern life requires a thoughtful approach that integrates faith into everyday experiences while acknowledging the practical demands and challenges of contemporary living. This balance helps ensure that Christian principles are lived out effectively amidst the complexities of modern society.

Start by defining core Christian values and understanding how they apply to daily life. Core values such as love, honesty, integrity, and compassion should guide your decisions and actions. Clearly identify these values and reflect on how they influence your daily interactions, choices, and priorities. Having a clear grasp of these principles will make it easier to apply them consistently.

Recognize and respect the demands of modern life. Acknowledge that contemporary life includes a variety of challenges and pressures, such as work commitments, social obligations, and technological advancements. While these realities may not always align perfectly with Christian values, it's important to navigate them thoughtfully. Understand that modern life may require flexibility, but this doesn't mean compromising on core values.

Integrate faith into daily routines by finding ways to incorporate Christian practices into everyday activities. For instance, you might start your day with a prayer or devotion, use Scripture to guide your decision-making, or look for opportunities to practice kindness and generosity. This integration helps maintain a constant reminder of your values while managing daily responsibilities.

Set priorities that reflect your faith. Determine what matters most and ensure that your Christian values are reflected in these priorities. This might involve making time for family, community service, or personal spiritual growth, even amidst a busy schedule. Balancing Christian values with modern life means finding ways to prioritize these aspects without neglecting your responsibilities.

Use modern tools and resources wisely. Technology and social media offer powerful tools for connecting with others and spreading positive messages, but they can also present challenges. Use these tools to promote and share Christian values, such as through uplifting content or supportive online communities. However, be mindful of how these tools impact your time and relationships, ensuring they serve as aids rather than distractions.

Address ethical dilemmas with a faith-based perspective. In situations where modern life presents ethical challenges, such as workplace decisions or social issues, apply Christian principles to guide your choices. Seek counsel from Scripture, prayer, and trusted mentors to navigate these dilemmas in a way that aligns with your values. Balancing faith with practical realities often involves seeking wisdom and making thoughtful, principled decisions.

Encourage open conversations about how to balance Christian values with modern life. Discuss these challenges with family members, friends, and fellow believers to gain different perspectives and support. Sharing experiences and strategies can provide practical insights and encouragement as you work to align your faith with everyday realities.

Practice grace and adaptability. Understand that maintaining this balance is an ongoing process and that there will be times when adjustments are necessary. Be flexible and compassionate with yourself and others as you strive to uphold your Christian values in various aspects of modern life. Recognize that imperfection is part of the journey, and seek to grow in faith through each experience.

Focus on the impact of your choices. Evaluate how your decisions and lifestyle affect your ability to live out Christian values. Consider whether your choices contribute to personal growth, positive relationships, and meaningful contributions to others. Strive to make decisions that enhance your faith and demonstrate Christian values in a practical and authentic way.

By blending these approaches, you can successfully navigate the complexities of modern life while staying true to your Christian values. This balance ensures that your faith remains a guiding force, enriching your daily experiences and interactions even as you engage with the demands and opportunities of contemporary living.

Conclusion

Reflecting on your parenting journey is a profound and meaningful practice that allows you to look back on the experiences, growth, and lessons learned while raising your children in a Christian home. This reflection can offer valuable insights and affirm the impact of your efforts as you continue to nurture and guide your family.

Begin by considering the goals and values you set at the beginning of your parenting journey. Think about the Christian principles that guided your decisions and actions. Reflect on how these values have influenced your approach to parenting and the way you interact with your children. Evaluate whether these goals are still relevant and if they need any adjustments based on your family's evolving needs.

Assess the progress your children have made and the growth they have achieved. Celebrate their accomplishments and milestones, whether big or small. Consider how your guidance and support have helped them develop into compassionate, confident, and Christ-centered individuals. Recognize and appreciate their unique strengths and the positive changes you have witnessed.

Reflect on the challenges and struggles you've faced along the way. Parenting is not without its difficulties, and it's important to acknowledge and learn from these experiences. Think about how you navigated tough situations and what you learned from them. Consider how these challenges have strengthened your faith and your ability to parent with grace and resilience.

Examine the effectiveness of your parenting strategies and practices. Consider which approaches worked well and which ones might need improvement. Reflect on the feedback and insights you received from your children and others. Use this reflection to make any necessary adjustments to your parenting style, ensuring that it aligns with your Christian values and meets the needs of your family.

Think about the relationships within your family. Reflect on how you have fostered communication, trust, and love. Consider the impact of family activities, shared experiences, and daily interactions on your family's bond. Reflect on how you have encouraged forgiveness, reconciliation, and unity, and how these efforts have shaped your family's dynamics.

Acknowledge the ways in which your own faith journey has influenced your parenting. Reflect on how your relationship with God has guided your decisions and actions. Consider the role of prayer, Bible study, and worship in your family life. Recognize how your spiritual growth has impacted your parenting and how it continues to shape your family's values and practices.

Look ahead to the future and envision the ongoing journey of parenting. Consider the new challenges and opportunities that may arise as your children grow and develop. Think about how you will continue to nurture their faith and character, and how you will adapt your parenting approach to meet their changing needs.

Reflect on the support systems and resources that have been helpful in your parenting journey. Consider the role of community, mentors, and other parents in your growth and development as a Christian parent. Acknowledge and appreciate the support you have received and think about how you can offer support and encouragement to others in their parenting journeys.

Ultimately, reflecting on your parenting journey is an opportunity to celebrate the progress you've made, learn from your experiences, and reaffirm your commitment to raising your children with faith and love. It's a chance to express gratitude for the blessings and growth you've experienced and to seek guidance and strength as you continue to nurture your family.

Encouragement for parents to continue growing in their faith and parenting skills.

Encouragement for parents to continue growing in their faith and parenting skills is essential for nurturing both your own spiritual journey and the development of your children. Parenting is an ongoing process, and remaining committed to growth and learning can enhance your effectiveness as a parent and strengthen your family's faith.

First, remember that growth in faith and parenting is a continuous journey. Just as your children are constantly developing and learning, so too are you. Embrace this journey with an open heart and mind. Seek opportunities for spiritual and personal growth through Bible study, prayer, and reflection. Understanding that you are on a lifelong path of growth can help you remain patient and open to change.

Engage in regular spiritual practices that enrich your faith. Set aside time for daily prayer and Bible reading, and involve your family in these practices. Strengthening your own relationship with God not only nurtures your spirit but also serves as a model for your children. Your commitment to spiritual growth can inspire them to develop their own faith practices.

Seek out resources and support to enhance your parenting skills. Attend parenting workshops, read books on Christian parenting, or join a parenting group within your church community. Learning from others and gaining new perspectives can provide valuable insights and practical strategies for effective parenting. Surround yourself with supportive friends and mentors who can offer encouragement and advice.

Be open to feedback and willing to adjust your approach as needed. Parenting is not a one-size-fits-all endeavor, and what works for one family may not work for another. Listen to your children's needs and concerns, and be flexible in adapting your parenting strategies. Reflect on your experiences and be willing to make changes that align with your values and your family's unique needs.

Celebrate your successes and acknowledge your efforts. Parenting is filled with challenges, but it's also full of moments of joy and achievement. Take time to recognize and appreciate the progress you and your children make. Celebrating these successes can boost your confidence and motivation, reinforcing your commitment to continued growth.

Remember that growth in faith and parenting also involves acknowledging and learning from mistakes. When things don't go as planned, approach these moments with humility and a willingness to learn. Use them as opportunities for growth and to model resilience and grace for your children. Demonstrating how to handle setbacks with faith and patience can be a powerful lesson for them.

Encourage open communication within your family. Create an environment where everyone feels comfortable sharing their thoughts, feelings, and concerns. Honest and respectful conversations can strengthen your family bond and provide insights into how you can better support each other. Engaging in these dialogues can also help you understand your children's perspectives and needs more deeply.

Finally, maintain a sense of hope and optimism. Parenting can be challenging, but keeping a positive outlook and trusting in God's guidance can provide strength and encouragement. Remember that you are not alone in your journey. Lean on your faith, seek support from your community, and trust that your efforts are making a meaningful impact.

Continuing to grow in your faith and parenting skills is a testament to your commitment to raising your children with love and integrity. By nurturing your own spiritual development and embracing opportunities for learning and growth, you can strengthen your family's foundation in Christ and foster an environment where both you and your children can thrive.

The importance of relying on God throughout the parenting process.

Relying on God throughout the parenting process is not just a spiritual practice; it's a deep, emotional anchor that provides strength, comfort, and guidance as you navigate the challenges and joys of raising your children. Parenting can be a journey filled with moments of joy, but also times of uncertainty and difficulty. Turning to God in these times can offer profound support and reassurance.

In the whirlwind of daily responsibilities, from managing school schedules to handling tantrums and teenage dilemmas, it's easy to feel overwhelmed. In those moments when you feel like you're at the end of your rope, it's vital to remember that you are not alone. God is a constant presence who offers wisdom, peace, and comfort. Allowing yourself to lean on God can transform those feelings of stress into a source of spiritual renewal. Your faith can act as a soothing balm, easing the burdens you carry and replacing anxiety with tranquility.

Turning to God through prayer provides a powerful means to express your deepest concerns and hopes. When you pray for your children, you're inviting divine guidance into their lives and yours. Each prayer becomes a channel through which God's wisdom and love can flow, giving you clarity and strength. This practice not only helps you navigate challenges with more grace but also builds a profound connection with God that fortifies your spirit. Knowing that you can always turn to God in prayer offers a comforting sense of reassurance and support.

When faced with difficult decisions or uncertain outcomes, relying on God allows you to surrender your worries and trust in a higher plan. This surrender is not about giving up but about finding peace in the knowledge that God's plan is greater than your own. It's about letting go of the need to control every aspect of your parenting and instead trusting in God's wisdom and timing. This shift in perspective can bring immense relief and help you to approach challenges with a calm and hopeful heart.

In moments of joy and celebration, acknowledging God's role in your parenting journey can deepen your sense of gratitude and connection. When you see your child achieve a milestone or show kindness, recognizing these as blessings and answers to prayer helps you stay centered in your faith. Celebrating these moments with a heart full of thankfulness can strengthen your bond with God and reinforce the values you strive to instill in your children.

Facing moments of failure or doubt is another critical area where relying on God can be transformative. Parenting does not come with a manual, and mistakes are inevitable. When you falter, turning to God can provide you with the reassurance that forgiveness and growth are always possible. God's grace is a powerful reminder that you can begin anew each day, learning from your experiences and continuing to strive toward being the parent you want to be.

Relying on God throughout the parenting process also means leaning on the support of your faith community. Engaging with others who share your beliefs can provide practical support and emotional encouragement. Your church community can be a source of wisdom, friendship, and shared experiences, helping you feel connected and supported in your journey.

Finally, teaching your children about the importance of relying on God sets a powerful example for them. When they see you turn to God in times of need, they learn the value of faith and trust in their own lives. This modeling of reliance on God teaches them resilience and hope, providing them with a spiritual foundation they can turn to throughout their lives.

Embracing God's presence throughout the parenting journey enriches your experience and deepens your connection to both your children and your faith. By allowing God to guide, comfort, and support you, you not only find strength for yourself but also create a nurturing environment where your children can grow in their own faith.

Final thoughts on raising Christ-centered children in a positive, loving environment.

Raising Christ-centered children in a positive, loving environment is a profound and fulfilling endeavor. As parents, you are entrusted with the sacred task of nurturing your children's spiritual, emotional, and moral growth. This journey is marked by a deep commitment to instilling values that reflect the love and teachings of Christ, creating a home where faith and love are the foundation of everyday life.

Creating a positive, loving environment means fostering a space where your children feel safe, valued, and understood. This begins with leading by example. Demonstrating kindness, patience, and respect in your interactions with others teaches your children how to embody these values themselves. When they witness love and grace in action within the family, they learn to replicate these behaviors in their own relationships.

In a Christ-centered home, love is more than just an emotion—it's an active choice that influences every decision and interaction. Encouraging open communication, practicing forgiveness, and showing empathy are vital aspects of a loving environment. These practices not only help to build a strong, supportive family bond but also reflect the teachings of Christ, who emphasized love, compassion, and understanding.

Instilling Christ-centered values involves more than just teaching about faith; it's about integrating these values into daily life. This can be achieved through prayer, Bible study, and engaging in acts of service. When you make these practices a regular part of your family routine, you help your children develop a personal relationship with Christ that will guide them throughout their lives.

Raising children in such an environment also means recognizing and nurturing their unique gifts and talents. Encouraging them to use these gifts to serve others and glorify God helps them understand their purpose and fosters a sense of fulfillment. Supporting their interests and passions while guiding them to use these in a Christ-centered way instills confidence and a strong sense of identity.

It's important to remember that while striving for a Christ-centered home is a noble goal, perfection is not the aim. There will be challenges and setbacks along the way, and that's part of the journey. What matters most is the commitment to continually seek God's guidance, to grow in faith, and to love unconditionally. Each day offers new opportunities to model Christ's love and grace, and to learn and grow as a family.

As you reflect on your parenting journey, take comfort in knowing that you are making a significant impact on your children's lives. Your efforts to create a loving, Christ-centered environment are shaping their values, their faith, and their futures. Trust that God is with you every step of the way, guiding and supporting you as you fulfill this important role.

In conclusion, raising Christ-centered children in a positive, loving environment is a journey of faith, commitment, and love. By leading with grace, integrating Christian values into daily life, and nurturing your children's spiritual and emotional growth, you are setting the stage for them to grow into compassionate, confident individuals who carry the light of Christ into the world.

© Tiffany Barker